Young, Gifted, and Black

Young, Gifted, and Black

PROMOTING HIGH ACHIEVEMENT AMONG

AFRICAN-AMERICAN STUDENTS

Theresa Perry

Claude Steele

Asa G. Hilliard III

BEACON

150

BEACON PRESS

BOSTON

Beacon Press
25 Beacon Street
Boston, Massachusetts 02108-2892
www.beacon.org

Beacon Press books
are published under the auspices of
the Unitarian Universalist Association of Congregations.

17   15 14

Portions of Theresa Perry's essay have appeared in Theresa Perry, "Situating
Malcolm X in the African American Native Tradition: Freedom for Literacy
and Literacy for Freedom," in *Teaching Malcolm X,* ed. Theresa Perry (New York:
Routledge Press, 1995); Theresa Perry, *Towards a Theory of African American
Achievement,* report no. 16. (Baltimore, Md.: Center on Families, Communities,
Schools, and Children's Learning, Johns Hopkins University, 1993); and Theresa
Perry, *An Interpretative Analysis of Martin Luther King Jr. v. Ann Arbor School Board
District Case* (unpublished manuscript, 1982).

This book is printed on acid-free paper that meets the uncoated paper
ANSI / NISO specifications for permanence as revised in 1992.

Composition by Wilsted & Taylor Publishing Services

Library of Congress Cataloging-in-Publication Data
Perry, Theresa.
        Young, gifted, and Black : promoting high achievement among African-
American students / Theresa Perry, Claude Steele, and Asa G. Hilliard III.
            p.   cm.
Includes bibliographical references.
        ISBN 978-0-8070-3105-6 (pbk. : alk. paper)
    1. African Americans—Education. 2. Academic achievement—United
States. 3. Educational equalization—United States.   I. Steele, Claude.
II. Hilliard, Asa G. III. Title.
        LC2717 .P47 2003
        371.82996'073—dc21

2002012009

CONTENTS

This book is a unique kind of collaboration. We come together as three scholars, with different disciplinary backgrounds and perspectives, to explore in new ways an issue of urgent importance and national debate: the experience and achievement of African-American students in schools.

We have written our essays separately. Each is the work of a single author, with a single voice. But we present our work together because we believe that we share key perspectives and purposes. We present our work together because we believe that juxtaposing our pieces one against the other will open up a space in the national conversation on this issue that is new and needed.

We share a general view that African-American students face challenges unique to them as students in American schools at all levels by virtue of their social identity as African Americans and of the way that identity can be a source of devaluaton in contemporary American society. We believe, as we all argue, that the contemporary conversation about African-American achievement ignores these social facts in ways that seriously distort the debate. And we all believe and argue that a proper understanding of the forces acting on African-American students points to a variety of educational practices that we know can mitigate these obstacles and promote excellent achievement.

Theresa identifies dilemmas of achievement facing African-American students as members of a group subject to an ideology of intellectual and cultural inferiority, and traces, historically and thematically, an indigenous African-American philosophy of achievement capable of addressing those dilemmas of achievement. Claude brings the perspective of empirical psychology to the question of achievement, identifying a phenomenon of stereotype threat that in a general way can be show to affect the achievement of people who are members of groups subject to stereotyped appraisals of their abilities; he, too, suggests that positive remedies follow from a proper understanding of this phenomenon. And Asa, after arguing against explanations that ignore the lived reality of ethnic identity in the United States, show us in detail teachers and programs who do not fail to produce excellence in academic achievement, regardless of the background of the students.

We do not agree on all matters, and we speak for ourselves. But we believe that readers who read our work together will see the connections between the pieces and hope that our collective work encourages both a new kind of national conversation and new research from a variety of potentially productive directions—historical, psychological, and educational. Our children deserve both.

THERESA PERRY

UP FROM THE PARCHED EARTH: TOWARD A THEORY OF AFRICAN-AMERICAN ACHIEVEMENT

Sylvia was strikingly beautiful. She had dark chocolate skin, coal black hair. She was built, too. The fact that she was smart had undoubtedly eluded her as she made her way through one of the city's public high schools. Her beauty and shapeliness hadn't. She was now a go-go dancer at one of the night spots in her Midwestern town. The story goes that one night, as she came down from the stage where she was dancing, she spotted the admissions counselor for the Educational Opportunity Program at one of the city's large private universities. "I want to go to school," she said. He responded, "You'll have to come and see me in my office to talk about how you can apply for the program." Five years later, this woman, who had graduated sixty-ninth out of eighty from what was then known as one of the worst high schools in the city, would have to decide between acceptances at the master's of public health programs at Yale, Harvard, and Boston University. She chose Yale, and upon graduation she became the first director of minority health care for her state.

I knew Tanya as a student when I taught at one of the two Black Catholic high schools in Birmingham, Alabama. My most persistent image is of her alternately checking out her pimples and fixing her hair, both with the aid of a small handheld mirror. I also knew that her family was often on the run from her abusive father, packing up in the night and going somewhere—anywhere—to get away. Thirty years later, at a reunion of graduates of the Educational Opportunity Program, now a professor of communications at a community college, she speaks, still with her southern accent, about how the program saved her life. She reminds us that at the time when her father was abusing her mother, nobody was talking much about domestic violence, especially in our southern Black community.

When Janice was about to go to law school, her oldest sister was about to go off to prison. We—that is, most of the program staff—had put money together (I think it came to five hundred dollars) so she could buy clothes for law school. "I got a nerve to be trying to go to law school with no clothes," she said, even as she excitedly showed us the clothes she had bought. She did attend and graduate from a top-twenty law school. She is now a practicing attorney. We now know that she could have also become a world-class runner, as we have over the years watched her consistently win track meets in her age group. But running was not then on her radar screen or ours, except as an activity she was attracted to as she tried to emulate the life and style of one of the program staff. At the same thirty-year reunion, the lawyer/runner reminisced about the wonderful events that came with being a member of the program's prelaw society. And more than once she reminded us that it was not simply the prelaw society, but the Third World Prelaw Society.

He was steadfast, hardworking; he wanted to be a doctor. His first-semester grades would have convinced most students and college faculty that, for him, being a physician was nothing more than a pipe dream. A summer at the New York City Department of Health working with a research team; participation in the Harvard Health Careers summer program (all arranged by program staff), along with supplementary instruction in math and science; a healthy dose of program rhetoric ("You guys are going to be the leaders of this community"); and five years later Jeremy enrolled in Harvard Medical School. His is now one of the largest community-based health clinics in his city. As he had always dreamed of doing, he is providing excellent health care to Latinos in the city, to his people.

There are the brothers, one a gynecologist, the other a history professor; Dwayne, the brilliant and compassionate assistant principal of an alternative high school; Gloria, by most accounts the most effective and the most progressive state legislator; John and David, entrepreneurs, one local, the other national. I could go on—but you get the point. The program these young people participated in, the Educational Opportunity Program, normalized high academic achievement for students who were mainly African-American, all first-generation college students, some of whom before entering the program did not have the skills, behaviors, beliefs, or identities required for high academic achievement. What was there about this program, this carefully constructed environment, that made it possible for program staff to routinely participate in the transformation of students into high academic achievers? How did the program help students redefine who they were and who they wanted to be? And perhaps most important, what were the tacit understandings, embraced and enacted by program staff, of what it would take for the mainly African-American and all first-generation college students to be high achievers?

I write this essay not only because of my experience as one of the individuals who worked in and helped to shape aspects of this program, but also because there are schools and programs all over the United States in which African-American youth routinely achieve at high levels. At these institutions, being working-class or poor, having parents who have not gone to college, being poorly prepared academically, being African-American—these variables are not impediments to academic achievement. Why are these institutions able to promote academic achievement among African-American students while so many other institutions are not? This is one of the questions that I will attempt to address.

I am also interested in trying to understand African-American school achievement, from the inside out, from the perspective of African-American youth as thinking, feeling, and social and intentional beings. What are the extra psychosocial and cognitive competencies that are required of African Americans, precisely because they are African-American, in order for them to achieve at high levels in school?

This essay is exploratory in nature. It will focus on the development of a theory of African-American achievement with sufficient power to explain and predict achievement across different environments. It is concerned with the development of a theory of African-

American achievement that is grounded in and predicated on an understanding of what it is we are asking African-American youth to do when we ask them to commit themselves, over time, to academic achievement in the context of the American school. In other words, I would argue that before we can theorize African-American school achievement, we need to have an understanding of what the nature of the task of achievement is for African Americans *as African Americans.*

For many educators and scholars, understandably, particularly those individuals who are committed to rejecting specious arguments about Black inferiority, this question is rarely addressed. It could even be a dangerous question. The focus on the specificity of the task of achievement for African Americans could easily be recast as a conversation about the intellectual deficiencies of African-American youth, and equally problematic, could undermine the liberal notion that progressive educational practices are color-blind.

The prevailing assumption among many educators is that the task of achievement for African Americans as a group is the same as it is for any other group. African-American children have to be able to do what all other children have to be capable of doing in order to achieve in American schools. These individuals proceed on the assumption that beyond individual differences—which they usually willingly concede particularize the task of learning—if you know what works for the white child, then you know what will work for the Black child. Indeed, there are generalizable competencies required of and embedded in the learning tasks students are asked to perform in school. But since learning is fundamentally contextual, I would argue that there are extra social, emotional, cognitive, and political competencies required of African-American youth, precisely because they are African-American, if they are to be able to commit themselves over time to perform at high levels in school. My argument is that the task of academic achievement for African Americans in the context of school in the United States of America is distinctive. In this essay, I will argue that the following dilemmas that many African-American students face make the task of achievement distinctive:

How do I commit myself to achieve, to work hard over time in school, if I cannot predict (in school or out of school) when or under what circumstances this hard work will be acknowledged and recognized?

How do I commit myself to do work that is predicated on a belief in the power of the mind, when African-American intellectual inferiority is so much a part of the taken-for-granted notions of the larger society that individuals in and out of school, even good and well-intentioned people, individuals who purport to be acting on my behalf, routinely register doubts about my intellectual competence?

How can I aspire to and work toward excellence when it is unclear whether or when evaluations of my work can or should be taken seriously?

Can I invest in and engage my full personhood, with all of my cultural formations, in my class, my work, my school if my teachers and the adults in the building are both attracted to and repulsed by these cultural formations—the way I walk, the way I use language, my relationship to my body, my physicality, and so on?

Will I be willing to work hard over time, given the unpredictability of my teachers' responses to my work?

Can I commit myself to work hard over time if I know that, no matter what I or other members of my reference group accomplish, these accomplishments are not likely to change how I and other members of my group are viewed by the larger society, or to alter our castelike position in the society? I still will not be able to get a cab. I still will be followed in department stores. I still will be stopped when I drive through certain neighborhoods. I still will be viewed as a criminal, a deviant, and an illiterate.

Can I commit myself to work hard, to achieve in a school, if cultural adaptation effectively functions as a prerequisite for skill acquisition, where "the price of the ticket" is separation from the culture of my reference group?

These are some of the dilemmas that African-American children, youth—and yes, even adults—face as they attempt to commit themselves to high academic achievement. It is these dilemmas, and more, that fundamentally alter the nature of the task of achievement for African Americans, rendering it distinctive, requiring extra social and cognitive competencies.

The task of achievement, I would argue, is distinctive for African Americans because doing school requires that you use your mind, and the ideology of the larger society has always been about questioning the mental capacity of African Americans, about questioning Black intellectual competence. The task of achievement requires investment over time, being "in there." It essentially demands that you be capable of bringing to the task who you are socially and emotionally and physically. And the only way you can do this is to bring your full sociocultural person to the task. The task of achievement requires that you and others believe that the intellectual work that you engage in affirms you as a social being and is compatible with who you are.

Further, and perhaps most important, evidence from history and the African-American narrative tradition suggests that African Americans have understood the distinctive nature of the task of achievement. And out of their lived experience, from slavery to the dismantling of segregated schools, they have developed and enacted a philosophy of education that was capable of providing answers to some of the aforementioned queries. This philosophy was freedom for literacy and literacy for freedom, racial uplift, citizenship, and leadership.

THE ACHIEVEMENT GAP AND THE CONTEMPORARY CONVERSATION ABOUT AFRICAN-AMERICAN ACHIEVEMENT

Writing on African-American school achievement at this time necessarily inserts one into the national conversation about the achievement gap. Many individuals, Black and white, practitioners, activists, educational leaders, and policy makers—situated in urban school districts; in progressive college towns; in upper-income, multiracial, liberal communities; in state houses and at the federal level—are engaged in a conversation about Black school achievement. The more things change, the more they stay the same—which is to say that the contemporary public conversations about Black school achievement, like virtually all past conversations about African-American school performance, remain focused on underachievement. Today it is termed the *achievement gap.*

There are aspects of the contemporary national conversation about the achievement gap that are problematic. Most prominently these include the failure to include alongside the data about African-American underachievement information about environments that promote high achievement among African Americans; the failure to acknowledge that this experiment with democracy, as it is applied to African Americans, is only about thirty years old. For if one considers the long and persistent denial and limiting of educational opportunity to African Americans, and African Americans' corresponding achievements, the historically grounded and educationally useful

question is, "How have African Americans, over generations, succeeded in maintaining their commitment to education and producing a leadership and intellectual class?"

The contemporary conversation about the achievement gap can
be characterized as follows: On whatever measure one uses, from the
SAT to the Stanford Nine, in school districts and schools across the
country, irrespective of political orientation, demographic characteristics, or per-pupil spending, there exists a gap between the academic
performance of Black and Latino students on the one hand and white
and Asian-American students on the other. This gap exists even between Black and white childrenwho ostensibly come from similar
social-class backgrounds and who attend the same school. As a matter
of fact, in a report prepared by the College Board, the most recent
analysis of SAT scores reveals that middle-class Black students perform no better than poor white students. This analysis also reveals that
the gap between Black middle-class and white middle-class students is
larger than the gap in the performance between poor white and poor
Black students (College Board 1999).

To make matters worse, especially for die-hard integrationists,
school districts that have prided themselves on being liberal, politically progressive towns, multiracial communities, good places for
Blacks to live, with excellent school systems, report the same achievement gap. Some of these communities, twelve to be exact, acknowledging the problem and determined to find and share solutions, have
organized themselves into what has come to be known as the Minority Achievement Network. The group includes college towns
Amherst, Massachusetts; Cambridge, Massachusetts; Madison, Wisconsin; Ann Arbor, Michigan; Evanston, Illinois; Berkeley, California; as well as Oak Park, Illinois; Shaker Heights, Ohio; Montclair,
New Jersey; and others. In the Nyack, New York, school district,
which has many of the same demographic characteristics as the districts that are part of the Minority Achievement Network, a group of
Black and white parents who for years have been trying to get the district to pay attention to the gap in achievement recently released a report that documented the underenrollment of Blacks in honors and
advanced-placement classes, their disproportionately higher rates of
suspension and enrollment in special-needs classes, and significantly
lower grade point averages.

Policy makers at the state and federal levels have also gotten into the mix. As a way to develop policies that might compel communities to address the achievement gap, several states, following Texas's lead, are considering requiring that school performance data be broken out by race and class. Further, and this is the rub, they are considering requiring that schools be evaluated not simply on average performance scores, but on whether a school has been able to promote achievement among Black, Latino, and poor children. The requirement that states and communities break out achievement data according to these criteria recently became an issue in congressional discussions about a proposed education bill, with members of the Senate worrying that a requirement to report data in this manner would cause schools that had previously been known as *good* schools now to be assessed as *underperforming* schools.

Notwithstanding the seemingly good intentions, the desire to improve African-American school performance, and the common-sense notion that the first step for a district committed to improving African-American academic performance is acknowledging that there is a problem, this conversation will almost surely reinforce the national ideology about Black intellectual inferiority. And, as such, the conversation is likely to be the location of yet another narrative that further undermines how African-American students are seen by others and by themselves. As Tasha Persaud noted in a *New York Times* article about the achievement gap (November 14, 1999), "If your doctor told you you can't run anymore, would you go out and run? If someone says again and again that you can't achieve, you don't even try." Although this conversation does not explicitly assert that Black students can't achieve, it is about their underachievement, and in a society where the dominant ideology is about Black intellectual inferiority, the conversation could have the effect that Tasha speaks about.

Furthermore, a review of newspaper articles about the achievement gap reveals that even as some of these articles identify tracking and teacher expectations as possible causes for underachievement, most give greater attention to variables that reside in Black families, students, and communities. The achievement gap is attributed to a peer culture that doesn't value achievement, and worse, one that associates school achievement with being white. Black students don't achieve because they spend less time doing homework and more time watching television than their white and Asian counterparts. Just as hip-hop culture is blamed for violence, it also is identified as one of the possible reasons for the achievement gap. The collective message is unfortunately similar to the assertion of a White Nyack parent, who in response to the report on Black underachievement commented, "The Nyack schools and [their] professionals are not responsible for the failures of the home, the conduct of absent child-bearers, or irresponsible and immoral and criminal parents . . . What are the homes like? What are the parents like? Do kids get a hot meal at the end of the day?" We have to face the fact that if we are going to have this public conversation about African-American student achievement, it will inevitably become a conversation that blames Black parents, Black students, and the Black community. The danger is that it will become yet another location for the recycling of the ideology of African-American moral, cultural, and intellectual deficiency.

The conversation about African-American achievement is problematic because it fails to begin with a careful examination of all aspects of the school, with an eye toward understanding *how* the school's day-to-day practices participate in the creation of underachievement. As a grandparent of a Head Start student in rural Louisiana observed years ago, "If the corn don't grow, nobody don't ask what's wrong with the corn."* We need to examine how race affects the reproduction of inequality in an allegedly open and integrated setting.

Which leads me to one of the possibilities contained in this conversation. As flawed as this conversation might be, it could provide a space for the introduction of race into public discussions about school and school reform. The conversation could provide a context that allows us to grapple with the notion that not all racial minorities occupy the same political position in this society, that their respective cultures have different meanings, that racial minorities occupy different spaces in the American psyche. The conversation might force an examination of the particular ways in which racism is embedded in "liberal" integrated educational settings. It might prompt discussions about Black achievement that foreground the racial and cultural identities of African Americans, discussions that do what I am attempting

*This story was told to me many years ago by Lisa Delpit. It emerged from her work with Head Start in Louisiana.

to do in this essay: focus on the particular nature of the task of achievement for African Americans, given our history, culture, and political location.

In part 1 of this essay, I will argue that over generations African Americans understood that the task of achievement was distinctive, and that out of their lived experience they developed a theory of knowledge and a philosophy of education that was capable of responding to the dilemmas of achievement embedded in this task. I will maintain that the philosophy of education—freedom for literacy and literacy for freedom, racial uplift, citizenship, and leadership— over the years has been encoded in the African-American narrative tradition. This philosophy of education was, at the same moment, both transcendent and grounded, and powerful enough to provide answers to those enduring dilemmas that plague African Americans as they have attempted to commit themselves to academic achievement.

In part 2, I will engage in a critical analysis of two theoretical models that have been used in discussing the school achievement of racial minorities: the cultural difference and social mobility theories. Like the philosophy of education developed by African Americans, these models foreground social group identity in discussing school achievement. The purpose of this analysis is to identify aspects of these theories that can be used in developing a theory of African-American achievement.

In part 3, after contrasting the task of achievement for African Americans in the pre– and post–Civil Rights eras, I will present an outline of a theory of African-American achievement. I will finally discuss the implications of this theory for educational practices and for families, schools, community-based organizations, and churches.

PART ONE

FREEDOM FOR LITERACY
AND LITERACY FOR FREEDOM:
THE AFRICAN-AMERICAN
PHILOSOPHY OF EDUCATION

The questions that are at the heart of the dilemma of schooling for African Americans, and perhaps for any group for whom there is not a predictable or rational relationship between effort and reward in the social, education, or economic spheres, are these: Why should one make an effort to excel in school if one cannot predict when and under what circumstances learning will be valued, seen, acknowledged? Why should one focus on learning in school if that learning doesn't, in reality or in one's imaginary community, have the capacity to affect, inform, or alter one's self-perception or one's status as a member of an oppressed group?

African Americans have historically given rich and elaborated answers to these questions. In *The Education of Blacks in the South, 1860–1935,* James Anderson unearths the answers that African Americans themselves provided—answers that were forged out of African Americans' early encounters with literacy and their struggles over time to acquire literacy and education in America. For African Americans, from slavery to the modern Civil Rights movement, the answers were these: You pursued learning because this is how you asserted yourself as a free person, how you claimed your humanity. You pursued learning so you could work for the racial uplift, for the liberation of your people. You pursued education so you could prepare yourself to lead your people.

Not coincidentally, this is the same message about literacy and education that literary scholars Henry Louis Gates and Robert Stepto have found encoded in the African-American narrative tradition, an impulse that Stepto summarizes as "freedom for literacy and literacy for freedom." I will argue that what Anderson and other historians have found in the historical record and what Gates and Stepto have seen in the African-American literary tradition are evidence for an indigenous African-American philosophy of education. I will further argue that this philosophy of education was powerfully implicated in motivating African Americans across generations to vigorously pursue education.

There is a tendency to see philosophy as an activity of specialized people, elites, who are usually ensconced in universities, far from the day-to-day activities of ordinary people. I am arguing that out of African Americans' collective experience with learning and education, and all that that implied, they developed a philosophy of education that was passed on in oral and written narratives. Moreover, narratives were not only the vehicles for passing on this philosophy, but they also had a discursive function. They were central to the identity formation of African Americans as intellectually capable people.

I want to help readers get a sense of the content and power of the African-American philosophy of schooling by doing a close reading of seven African-American narratives. My goal is to make palpable the feelings, the meanings, and the significance African Americans have attached to schooling and learning, to make visible their indigenous philosophy of education. These narratives—some literature and some not—allow us to see how this philosophy of education found expression in the real lives of people, or at least in their memory. The two slave narratives and the five contemporary narratives that I have chosen to discuss are representative of the experiences of African Americans during slavery and in the twentieth century. But I could have just as easily chosen other narratives, as there are dozens of narratives in which one can find the same messages, from Booker T. Washington's *Up from Slavery* to Vernon Jordan's recently published *Vernon Can Read*.

My primary argument is that this indigenous and operative philosophy of learning and schooling was capable of developing and sustaining the desire for learning in a people for whom educational accomplishment was not necessarily linked to comparable rewards, primarily because education was so tied to the identity of African Americans as a free people. I further argue that this philosophy was passed on in both oral and written narratives and institutionalized in the school communities created by African Americans. I will end part 1 of this essay by reflecting on how this discussion might inform contemporary conversations about African-American school achievement and what the historic African-American philosophy of education can contribute toward the development of a contemporary theory of African-American school achievement.

SLAVE NARRATIVES AND AN AFRICAN-AMERICAN PHILOSOPHY OF LEARNING

Law and custom made it a crime for enslaved men and women to learn or teach others to read and write. And yet slave narratives uniformly recount the intensity of the slaves' and ex-slaves' desire for literacy, the barriers they encountered in becoming literate, and what they were willing to endure in order to become literate. Even the threat of beating, amputation, or death did not quell the slaves' desire for literacy. According to the testimony of one slave, "The first time you was caught trying to read or write you was whipped with a cow hide the next time with a cat-o-nine and the third time they cut the first joint offen your forefinger" (Cornelius 1991, 66).

There are the stories of slaves who were hanged when they were discovered reading, and of patrollers who went around breaking up Sunday meetings where slaves were being taught to read, beating all of the adults who were present. Slaves cajoled white children into teaching them, trading marbles and candy for reading lessons. They paid large sums of money to poor white people for reading lessons and were always on the lookout for time with the blue black speller (a school dictionary), or for an occasion to learn from their masters and mistresses without their knowing.

For the slaves, literacy was more than a symbol of freedom; it *was* freedom. It affirmed their humanity, their personhood. To be able to read and write was an intrinsic good, as well as a mighty weapon in the slave's struggle for freedom. Literate slaves filed legal petitions, protesting and challenging their enslavement; they forged passes for themselves and others, thus allowing escape from the horrors of slavery. Literate slaves read newspapers and pamphlets and kept themselves and the slave community informed about the antislavery movement and the war. Denmark Vesey, David Walker, Nat Turner, and other literate slaves led rebellions and wrote pamphlets and tracts denouncing and exposing the slave system. They read the Bible, interpreting its message in a way that supported resistance and rebellions.

While learning to read was an individual achievement, it was fundamentally a communal act. For the slaves, literacy affirmed not only their individual freedom but also the freedom of their people. Becoming literate obliged one to teach others. Learning and teaching were two sides of the same coin, part of the same moment. Literacy was not something you kept for yourself; it was to be passed on to others, to the community. Literacy was something to share.

Frederick Douglass
The Narrative of the Life of Frederick Douglass can be viewed as a representative slave narrative text, one that captures with unusual clarity and power the meaning of learning and literacy for African Americans. Frederick Douglass had the good fortune of having a mistress, Mrs. Auld, who began the process of teaching him to read. Douglass describes Mrs. Auld as a woman who was different from any other white woman he had known, a difference he attributed to both her previously having never been in charge of slaves and her having worked on her own for a living. Mrs. Auld—at least for a time—did not require or expect of slaves the usual kind of servile behavior. And yet this seemingly humane individual would ultimately be transformed by the slave system, eventually becoming as intent as other slaveholders on creating impediments to Douglass's pursuit of literacy.

When Mrs. Auld's husband found her teaching Douglass to read, he demanded that she stop immediately. What was significant in this encounter was not simply the vehemence and force with which Mr. Auld forbade his wife to teach Douglass, but the reasons he gave for this prohibition—reasons that assuredly were heard time and time again by enslaved Africans, reasons that ultimately came to shape the meaning that Douglass and other Africans attached to literacy, learning, reading, writing, and education.

According to Mr. Auld, education would "spoil a nigger," make him unfit to be a slave, make him discontent, unhappy, and unmanageable. Mr. Auld's lecture and lesson on the incompatibility of slavery and education profoundly affected Douglass. Indeed, out of Douglass's lived experiences, out of his interaction with his mistress and master, emerges his philosophy of education. And against the backdrop of this prohibition, Douglass is unequivocal about the meaning, the power, and the possibilities he and other Africans will come to attach to reading and writing.

In the African-American narrative tradition, few individuals articulate with such clarity the historic African-American philosophy of schooling, of learning: freedom for literacy and literacy for freedom. Consider the words of Douglass:

> From that moment, I understood the pathway from slavery to freedom. It was just what I wanted, and I got it at a time when I least expected. Whilst I was saddened by the thought of losing the aid of my kind mistress, I was gladdened by the invaluable instruction which, by merest accident, I had gained from my master. Though conscious of the difficulty of learning without a teacher, I set out with high hope and a fixed purpose, at whatever cost of trouble, to learn how to read. The decided manner with which he spoke, and strove to impress his wife with the evil consequences of giving me instruction served to convince me that he was deeply sensible of the truths he was uttering. It gave me the best assurance that I might rely with the utmost confidence on the results which, he said, would flow from teaching me to read. What he most feared, that I most desired. What he most loved, that I most hated. That which to him was a great evil, to be carefully shunned, was to me a great good, to be diligently sought, and the argument which he so warmly waged, against my learning to read, only seemed to inspired me with a desire and determination to learn. (Douglass 1968, 47–48)

And, of course, the seemingly humane Mrs. Auld complied with the demands of her husband. She was, in fact, ultimately transformed by the slave system, becoming even more determined than Mr. Auld to prevent Douglass from learning to read. If she saw Douglass reading a newspaper, she would, with great fury, grab it out of his hand. If Douglass was alone in a room for a significant period of time, suspecting that he was reading, she would come and look for him. Her determination to keep Douglass from reading was matched and exceeded by Douglass's determination to learn how to read and write. Douglass created opportunities, openings, when there appeared to be none. He made friends with poor white children, and whenever he went on errands, he took his book and some bread (which was readily available at the Auld house), which he gave to the children in exchange for reading lessons.

Once he had learned to read, Douglass read books that deepened his understanding of slavery and arguments against it. As Mr. Auld had predicted, the more he read, the more restless, discontent, and unhappy he became. His desire for freedom became unquenchable. About the impact of reading on him, Douglass says,

> As I read and contemplated the subject, . . . the very discontent which Master Hugh had predicted would follow my learning to read had already come to torment and sting my soul to unutterable anguish. The silver trump of freedom had aroused my soul to eternal wakefulness. Freedom now appeared, to disappear no more forever. It was heard in every sound, and seen in every thing. . . . I saw nothing without seeing it, I heard nothing without feeling it. It looked from every star, it smiled in every calm, breathed in every wind, and moved in every star. (53)

Douglass demonstrated the same persistence and intensity in learning to write as he had in learning to read. His vision was that learning to write would eventually enable him to write himself a pass, to be used in his escape to freedom. Douglass describes his learning to write as a "long and tedious effort" (56).

Eventually Douglass would be moved to a smaller plantation. In this new setting, after noting the desire to read in some of his enslaved brethren, and nurturing it in others, he organized a Sabbath school, which met on Saturdays, and during the winter sometimes as often as three times a week. In reflecting on the deep satisfaction he experienced in teaching other enslaved Africans, Douglass confirms that he indeed saw education as tied to the liberation and racial uplift of his people: "They were great days to my soul. The work of instructing my fellow slaves was the sweetest engagement which I was ever blessed. . . . I taught them because it was the delight of my soul to be doing something that looked like bettering the condition of my race" (88).

It was a small group of individuals from Douglass's Sabbath school who would eventually participate with Douglass in a plan to escape slavery. As Douglass had imagined, forging passes for those involved would be central to the escape plan. Although this escape to the north was foiled, Douglass would eventually succeed in escaping slavery, become active in the antislavery movement, and write three narratives of his life as an enslaved African. His narratives, like other slave narratives, became a vehicle for exposing the inhumanity of the system of slavery and arguing for its abolition. Perhaps most important, they allowed him to assert himself as a literate and literary person, as a human and as a free man.

Harriet Jacobs

Feminist literary scholars have argued that Stepto's and Gates's contention that the theme embedded in the slave narratives, freedom for literacy and literacy for freedom, cannot be so easily applied to narratives written by female slaves. Harriet Jacobs's *Incidents in the Life of a Slave Girl* is presented as an example of a female slave narrative whose central theme is the struggle for freedom and home. However, I would argue that the theme of freedom for literacy and literacy for freedom is as central to Jacobs's narrative as it is to Douglass's.

Harriet Jacobs was born in Edenton, North Carolina, in 1813. Her mother died when she was six years of age. She grew up under the watchful eye and love of her grandmother. Although Harriet was enslaved until she was fifty years old, her grandmother, who was also a slave, had her own home and was able to make money for herself and her family by selling crackers that she made at night.

Harriet Jacobs was taught to read and write to read by her mistress. At eleven years of age, after the death of her mistress, Harriet was willed to her mistress's two-year-old daughter. As Harriet matured, she would be constantly sexually threatened by her young mistress's father, Dr. Flint. Jacobs is clear in her narrative and letters that she is writing her narrative so that she can illuminate the particular ways in which slavery affects the enslaved female, as mother and woman. As punishment for resisting the sexual advances of Dr. Flint and refusing to become his concubine, Harriet is sent to live on a nearby plantation with Dr. Flint's son. While there, she learns that Dr. Flint is planning to arrange for her two children, who are living with her grandmother, to come to live with her on the plantation. Harriet desperately doesn't want her children to live on the plantation. She is especially opposed to having her daughter come to live on the plantation because of the particular dangers that her daughter will eventually face as a girl as she grows up. Harriet reasons that if she were to run away, her master would not send her children to the plantation, since they would be too much trouble without her. She does run away, and she is right. Dr. Flint gives up on the idea of sending her children to the plantation. Eluding capture by her master for seven years, she lives in her grand-mother's house, in a crawl space above the storeroom, "nine feet long and seven feet wide . . . [with] the highest part . . . [being] three feet high, and sloped down abruptly to the loose board floor." Jacobs's literacy is central to her being able to elude capture by her master. She writes letters to her master, Dr. Flint, and to her grandmother, and ar-ranges for these letters to be mailed from New York. She is thus able to convince her master that she has gone north. This act of deception allows her to live under the nose of her master for a long time, while shifting the search for her to another location. Her ploy works. Even before she actually does escape to New York, Dr. Flint travels to New York in search of her.

While Jacobs is imprisoned in this crawl space, she occupies her-self with reading, sewing, and practicing her writing. Once she es-capes to the north, she is employed as a nursemaid. She does this work so that she not only can take care of herself but also can send her chil-dren to school. While working as a nursemaid, at night and in secret, she begins to write about her life as an enslaved woman. Even though her employer is not proslavery, she still feels that she must write at night in secrecy in order to avoid ridicule. In her letters she is clear that, whatever her limitations in terms of literacy, she wants to write her own story. Thus I would assert that literacy is critical to Harriet's escape, to her being able to secure her freedom. She is occupied with literacy even while she is imprisoned, and ultimately her literacy allows her to tell her own story about her life as an enslaved woman, hoping that this narrative may motivate white women in the North to fight for abolition of slavery.

CONTEMPORARY NARRATIVES

Malcolm X

The African-American philosophy of schooling—freedom for liter-acy and literacy for freedom—finds expression not only in slave narratives but in other narratives written from emancipation to the contemporary period. There is perhaps no contemporary narrative that captures the African-American philosophy of schooling as powerfully as does the *Autobiography of Malcolm X*.

The *Autobiography of Malcolm X* captures with great poignancy the recurring ways that the dilemma of achievement is manifested in contemporary society, and in an allegedly open, integrated context. The narrative also provides an answer to the dilemma of achievement, though not apparent at the time when the dilemma is experienced by Malcolm, an answer that resonates with and is just as powerful as the one contained in the narrative of Frederick Douglass.

Malcolm X's narrative asks and answers those questions that contemporary educators of African-American students skittishly avoid but must inevitably confront: Why become literate in contemporary America? Why become proficient at reading and writing? Why should African-American youth take school seriously if they cannot predict when and under what circumstances their intellect or intellectual work is likely to be taken seriously? Why should African-American youth commit themselves to doing outstanding intellectual work if—because of the marker of skin color—this work is likely to be undervalued, evaluated differently from that of whites, or ignored? Why work hard at school, or at anything else for that matter, if these activities are not inextricably linked to and address one's status as a member of a historically oppressed people?

The *Autobiography of Malcolm X* takes up these questions and provides an answer, *the* answer that has become embedded in African Americans' collective consciousness and narrative tradition: Read and write yourself into freedom! Read and write to assert your identity as a human! Read and write yourself into history! Read and write as an act of resistance, as a political act, for racial uplift, so you can lead your people well in the struggle for liberation! (Stepto 1991; Davis and Gates 1990; Cornelius 1991; Anderson 1988; Fairclough 2001).

The dilemma, *why become literate?* is captured in an encounter between Malcolm X and his high school English teacher, Mr. Ostrowski. Reflecting on his high school performance, Malcolm remembers himself as an excellent student who was academically near the top of his class. He had received some of his best grades from Mr. Ostrowski, who had quite a reputation among students for being a careful, thoughtful, and supportive adviser. Mr. Ostrowski routinely encouraged white students with nonstellar academic records and those from working-class backgrounds to strike out on their own, to take risks, to extend themselves in new directions. Malcolm, however, did not receive this kind of encouragement from Mr. Ostrowski. It was as if his achievement as one of the best students in the class were invisible. What was salient was his status, his identity as a "Black Person."

Having been queried by Mr. Ostrowski about his career goals, Malcolm—admittedly not knowing what prompted his answer—replied that he wanted to be a lawyer. Mr. Ostrowski quickly disabused Malcolm of this notion, remarking, "Malcolm, one of life's needs is for us to be realistic. Don't misunderstand me now, we are here like you, you know that. . . . But you have to be realistic being a nigger" (34).

Malcolm recalls how, after this encounter, he turned away from whites. He became detached from them at school and at the restaurant where he worked. He even became detached from the Swerlins, the couple who ran the detention home where he lived. According to Malcolm, this encounter changed everything for him, and the white people around him knew it. Noticing the change in his attitude, they repeatedly asked him what was wrong. Malcolm's academic achievement, his status as one of the best students in the class, had not prepared him for Mr. Ostrowski's reaction to his achievement. He was "Black," and his achievement did not neutralize this reality. Malcolm reflected on his encounter with Mr. Ostrowski: "I realized that whatever I wasn't, I was smarter than nearly all of those white kids. But apparently I was not intelligent enough in their eyes to become whatever I wanted to be" (44).

It was not inevitable that Mr. Ostrowski's attempt to dissuade Malcolm from becoming a lawyer would cause him to lose interest in school. The interaction might have had a different ending. A colleague of mine often speaks about her two boys, who were among a few African Americans integrating a predominantly white school. She speaks about the different reactions they had to the racist practices and comments that were commonplace at the school. Regarding one of the boys, she says the racist comments "just stuck to him," affected him so profoundly that she had to take him out of the school. Similar racist incidents and comments just "rolled off the back" of another boy. Malcolm's school career might have been different had he had a different temperament. It might have been different had he, like lawyer/writer Gwendolyn Parker and former surgeon general Joycelyn Elders, whose narratives I will examine, been a member of a community that institutionalized and passed on the African-American epistemology of schooling—freedom for literacy and literacy for freedom. It might have been different if, at that time, he had been surrounded by family members who, like world-renowned neurosurgeon Ben Carson's mother, in another narrative I will examine, systematically passed on to him a counternarrative about his intellectual abilities.

It is important to note that even though Malcolm was separated from his family when the incident occurred, at an earlier point in his life his mother had passed on to him the importance of literacy and reading. According to interviews with family and friends, in the evening his mother would read to him and his siblings the *Garvey Papers* and *The Negro World*. When they were young children, they would gather around the stove and sing the alphabet, as well as math and French songs.

While as a schoolboy Malcolm was not able to offer a meaningful answer to the dilemma of achievement, as an adult, while in prison, he would offer what might be considered one of the most compelling answers contained in a contemporary narrative to the question *"why literacy?"* The answer begins and unfolds with his development as a literate person.

Malcolm's first movement toward literacy was inspired by Bimbi, an older Black prisoner who, according to Malcolm, was like a "walking encyclopedia." With Black and white prisoners gathered around, Bimbi would hold court, speaking eloquently about almost any subject. Bimbi was the first man whom Malcolm had met for whom words were power. It was not simply Bimbi's knowledge that motivated Malcolm in his quest for literacy, but also his ability to communicate this knowledge in a way that could capture the attention of a group. Here we have an expanded definition of literacy and its power to liberate. Becoming literate, for Malcolm, was a way to claim one's humanity, to equip oneself with a weapon to be used in the struggle for freedom. To be literate also included what you could do with your

knowledge—with words—whether you could use words to motivate
people to action, persuade people of the truth of your assertions, or inspire others to become literate.

Although the example of Bimbi, who was extremely knowledge-
able and a great orator, was motivating, it was Malcolm's spiritual and
political conversion to the Nation of Islam that occasioned his dogged, relentless quest to become learned. Malcolm wanted to be able to
communicate more effectively with the honorable Elijah Muhammad, to be as articulate in his letters to Elijah as he had been in the
streets as a hustler. He realized almost immediately that in order to become an effective communicator, he needed to improve both his pen-
manship and his vocabulary. Malcolm reflects:

> I must have written that one-page letter to him [Elijah Muhammad] over
> and over. I was trying to make it both legible and understandable. I practi-
> cally couldn't read my handwriting myself. It shames me even to remem-
> ber it. (185)

> The things I felt I was pitifully unable to express in the one-page letter
> that went every other day to Mr. Muhammad. (186)

> I became increasingly frustrated at not being able to express what I
> wanted to convey in the letters that I wrote, especially those to Elijah
> Muhammad. In the street, I had been the most articulate hustler out there
> —I had commanded attention when I said something. But now, trying
> to write simple English, I not only wasn't articulate, I wasn't even func-
> tioning. How would I sound writing slang, the way I would say it, some-
> thing such as, "look, daddy, pull me your coat about a cat, Elijah Muham-
> mad—?" (197)

Malcolm also wanted to be able to pass on his newly acquired religious and political knowledge to those he knew from the streets. He
wanted to acquire knowledge that would support and substantiate the
teachings of the Nation of Islam. And perhaps most important, he
wanted to confront those in power about the injustices that were per-
petrated upon Black people.

> I have never been one for inaction. Everything I have ever felt strongly
> about, I have done something about. I guess that's why, unable to do any-
> thing else, I soon began to write people I had known in the hustling

world, such as Sammy the pimp, John Hughes, the gambling house owner, and the thief, Jump Steady, and several dope peddlers. I wrote them all about Allah and Islam, and Mr. Elijah Muhammad. . . .

Later on, I even wrote to the mayor of Boston, to the governor of Massachusetts, and to Harry S. Truman. They never answered; they probably never saw my letters. I hand scratched to them how the white man's society was responsible for the black man's condition in this wilderness of North America. It was because of my letters that I happened to stumble upon starting some kind of home-made education. (196–97)

Malcolm's realization that he needed to improve his writing and acquire more knowledge led him to begin the arduous task of copying the entire dictionary, memorizing each word that he did not know. This activity allowed him to acquire the word knowledge that he needed to document the teachings of the Nation of Islam and to begin to understand better the complexities of the situation of Black people in the United States and throughout the world. Malcolm also read in subject areas that were not immediately relevant to either the life or the life chances of Black people, or of nonwhite people. What follows are some of Malcolm's thoughts about literacy:

Anyone who has read a great deal can imagine the new world that opened. Let me tell you something: from then until I left the prison, in every free moment I had, if I was not reading in the library, I was reading on my block. You couldn't have gotten me out of books with a wedge. Between Mr. Muhammad's teachings, my correspondence, my visitors, . . . and my reading of books, months passed without my even thinking about being imprisoned, in fact, up to then, I had never been so truly free in my life. (199)

Ten guards and the wardens couldn't have torn me out of those books. Not even Elijah Muhammad could have been more eloquent than those books in providing indisputable proof that the collective white man had acted like a devil in virtually every contact he had with the world's collective non-white man. (204)

Mr. Muhammad, to whom I was writing daily, had no idea of what new world had opened up to me through my efforts to document his teachings and books. (206)

I have often reflected upon the new vistas that reading opened for me. I knew right there in prison that reading had changed forever the course of my life. . . . My home-made education gave me, with every additional book that I read, a little bit more sensitivity to the deafness, and blindness that was affecting the Black race in America. (206)

If I weren't out here every day, battling the white man, I could spend the rest of my life just reading, just satisfying my curiosity—because you can hardly mention anything I am not curious about. (207)

Malcolm was passionate, single-minded, and persistent in his pursuit of literacy. He recalls how, while in prison, after the lights were out, he would read until three o'clock in the morning, stopping only minutes before the guard made his hourly rounds, and starting again after the guard passed his cell. The description of a slave's quest for literacy contained in one of the slave narratives can be aptly applied to Malcolm: "He slipped so he could read" (Cornelius 1991, 65).

Indeed, books were Malcolm's alma mater, and they opened a whole new world for him. Reading was not a casual endeavor; it consumed his life, took up every free moment—even those that should reasonably have been reserved for sleep. The object of his inquiry was Black people, but he also wanted to learn about the world at large. According to those who knew him, there was absolutely nothing about which he was not curious. By Malcolm's own assessment, reading transformed his life, made him free, even as he was imprisoned. For Malcolm, as for the slaves, literacy was not something to be kept for yourself; it was to be passed on. This attitude toward literacy and learning is captured in the comments of Yuri, an activist and associate of Malcolm's. According to her, "Malcolm had a Liberation School. . . . One thing Malcolm said was, 'A school is not four walls and a roof. It is whenever you get one person willing to teach and one who's willing to learn,' and he said that all of us should play both sides—sometimes we are teachers, and sometimes we are students."

Malcolm's *Autobiography* is an iconic text that indicates the power of the African-American philosophy of education not only as a nineteenth-century vehicle for liberation, but as a contemporary one. What is remarkable—and what I hope to illustrate—is that Malcolm's story, though famous and influential, is by no means unique. With a variety of inflections, but with surprising consistency, dozens of contemporary autobiographical narratives contain the same lessons and message about education.   ★   ★   ★

For my purpose I have chosen to examine the narratives of Joycelyn Elders, the former U.S. surgeon general; Haki Madhubuti, formerly Don L. Lee and possibly the most famous poet of the Black arts movement of the late sixties and early seventies; Gwendolyn Parker, a Radcliffe graduate and lawyer-turned-writer, whose most recent works include *Trespassing* and *These Long Bones;* Septima Clark, a civil rights activist who played a major role in the establishment of the Citizenship Schools; and Ben Carson, the young brilliant neurosurgeon, author of *The Gifted Hands,* who became director of pediatric neurosurgery at Johns Hopkins at the age of thirty–three.

As a group, these individuals represent the diversity of the African-American community. The group includes a member of the Black elite and representatives of the working poor. These individuals were raised in the rural South and in the urban North, in two-parent and single-parent families. Their birth dates range from the end of the nineteenth century to the mid-twentieth century. Notwithstanding the diversity of geographic location, family configuration, and social class, the individuals whose lives are chronicled in these narratives had the same message passed on to them about the power and importance of reading and education. For all of them, education was how you claimed your humanity, struck a blow for freedom, worked for racial uplift, and prepared yourself for leadership.

Joycelyn Elders
Joycelyn Elders, the oldest of eight children, was born in the small rural town of Schaal, Arkansas, home to no more than ninety residents. Her autobiography paints a picture of a life lived on the land, the life of a Black southern sharecropper family in the first half of the twentieth century. It was a life of hard work in the fields from morning until night, a life punctuated by acute anxiety about the threats of floods and locusts, by worry that the hard work of the entire family would not be enough for mere subsistence. Elders remembers her father as a man who worked all the time, a man "consumed with work." Her entire family—mother and siblings—all worked in the field alongside her father. Joycelyn herself was head of a work crew from the time she was five until she left for college. Aside from working in the field, whenever her father had time, he also hunted for raccoons. Selling raccoon skins was one of the few sources of cash for the family, cash

that her father would squirrel away and eventually use to purchase eighty acres of land, thus freeing the family from the bondage of sharecropping.

As Elders narrates a life of struggle for subsistence that engaged the entire family, she tells us that her earliest and clearest memory is of her mother teaching her to read. As constant as her mother's prayers was the refrain that accompanied her reading lessons: "You got to get a good start." Elders recalls that by age five she had become a good reader. Having mastered the primer her mother used to teach her to read, her reading material then became the Bible and the farmer's newspaper, *The Grit,* to which her father subscribed. And her mother moved on with her reading lessons to her next oldest sibling.

If Joycelyn uses the constancy of her mother's prayers as a way to capture the persistence of her mother's message about the importance of reading and learning, she uses the image of a drumbeat to similarly characterize her grandmother's message about education. Elders says, "Grandma Minnie was another one who was constantly at me. 'You've got to get a education.' That was her refrain like a drumbeat" (Elders and Chanoff 1996, 51).

Another variation of the message about the importance of education that Elders frequently heard from her mother and grandmother was "You got to get an education if you want to be 'somebody.'" Elders explains what "somebody" meant. Her grandmother and mother were not talking about having a particular career or aspiring to a particular profession. According to Elders, "Going to college wasn't something that ever occurred to any of us. The only thing we ever saw people doing was work: I'm talking about physical labor. Everyone we knew was in overalls driving mules" (13). As it did for the enslaved and recently freed men and women, to be "somebody" meant to be a human, to be a person, to be counted, to be the opposite of a slave, to be free. Thus, even as Joycelyn and other children in the community were urged to get an education so they could "be somebody," Elders recalls how the minister of her church, in an attempt to give them hope, would preach that they *were* "somebody." They were somebody, and yet education and reading was, as it was for the slaves, another way for them to affirm their identity as free men and women.

As if anticipating the contemporary need to exceptionalize the lives of successful African Americans, Elders is quick to remind us that her family was not the only family that had passed these messages about education on to their children and other people's children. In this context, she reflects on the origin of African Americans' deep beliefs about education:

> This wasn't just us. It was all of the people around us. One reason for this general reverence for learning was that none of the families in Schaal and Tollette and Bright Star was very far removed from slavery. Their great-grandparents, or grandparents, sometimes even their parents had been born at a time when they were not allowed to go to school. They weren't permitted to know how to read. They were the immediate descendents of people who had huddled up in undercover schools in churches or hidden out with a teacher in the woods so they could learn their letters. So when my father came along, he was going to get as much schooling as he possibly could, even though he was a full-time hand from the time he could lift something or carry something else. (52)

To know what a people believes, one should of course pay attention to what they say, what they portray in music, poetry, and stories. But one also pays attention to the choices a people make day in and day out, most critically to the decisions made under extreme circumstances. Often, just for her family to make it economically, Joycelyn and her brothers had to miss school to work in the fields. This was so embarrassing for Joycelyn that she would lie, telling her teacher that she just didn't feel like coming to school. In retrospect, Joycelyn was sure that her teachers knew why she had missed school. Even as the circumstances of her life sometimes forced her family to keep the children home from school to work in the fields, her parents made a decision that the children would always be in school when they had exams, would always have their books at home to do their schoolwork, and would always have time in the evening after a day in the field to do their schoolwork.

It is useful to spend a little time reflecting on the conditions under which Joycelyn and the other children in her community went to school, conditions that could surely have extinguished the desire for learning in individuals and in the African-American community, if not for the meaning African Americans had come to attach to learning. As an elementary student, Joycelyn attended a two-room schoolhouse, with students aged five to thirteen. With no desks or chairs in the school, the students sat on long wooden benches. They did their work on their laps, writing on single sheets of paper the teacher would tear from a tablet. Like many Black students of that era, with no high school in her community, Joycelyn attended a regional high school. Along with students from the surrounding communities (fifteen to twenty busloads), she was bused to the regional segregated high school for Black students. The buses were not your typical school buses, nor were they provided by the school system. These buses were built by the local communities, and they were all similar to the one the Elders family traveled to school in. Elders describes the bus that Mr. George Ogden had built for her community,

> George had taken a truck chassis and built a long flatbed onto it. On this flatbed he had constructed a rectangular wooden box, cutting out areas where you would ordinarily expect to find windows. . . . On these cutouts, George had nailed wire screenings over these openings, so children wouldn't fall out, and . . . fixed on rolls of burlap that could be lowered over the openings from the outside, like window shades. . . . Inside the box the seating was also homemade, rigged up wooden benches. (46)

What is important here is that, in face of the system's failure to provide either a local high school or transportation to the regional high school, the community improvised, found a way to create a transportation system so that their children could have a high school education. The willingness of Elders's community, and other African-American communities, to do whatever needed to be done in order to provide education for their children is captured again and again in the historical record and African-American narratives. In the oral narratives of African Americans' experience of Jim Crow we learn how the people in one community persuaded the school committee to put up half the money for the purchase of land for a playground by agreeing to contribute the other half. After the land had been purchased, a member of the community who had grading equipment landscaped the land. In another community, families routinely sent their children to school with the wood that was needed to heat the school. Another community bought the land and built a house for the principal. Here we have evidence of African Americans' willingness to tax themselves to provide whatever was needed so that their children could be educated. These are just some of the ways African-American communities around the country lived out the African-

American philosophy of education. These were not the actions of exceptional Black communities. These actions were part of the taken-for-granted activities of Black communities throughout the South.

What is remarkable is that these conditions—the conditions of the school, the circumstances of their lives—did not cause Joycelyn or her community to lose interest in schooling, to be less committed to education. Listen to how Joycelyn describes her reaction to the context within which she pursued an education: "The fact is that I liked learning too much to be put off. I didn't just like it, I loved it. A good part of that feeling came from my family. I had heard preaching on this subject from all sides from the time I could remember. I don't think it's any accident that my mother is there in my first memory teaching me to read."

It was time for Joycelyn to go off to college, and as valedictorian of her class she had been awarded a full-tuition scholarship to Philander Smith College, a historically Black college. As the time for her to leave approached, she knew that as much as her parents wanted her to go they were in deep conversation with each other about whether they could afford for her to go, could afford for her not to be a member of the work crew. It was Joycelyn's grandmother who stepped in and was the final arbiter and said that she was going to college, affirming what was ultimately important.

Even after Joycelyn had received a tuition scholarship, and after the decision had been made by the family that she would go to Philander Smith, she still did not have enough money for transportation. Elders recalls how the entire family went into the field early, before the harvest season officially began, to work to get money for her transportation. One of her most poignant memories is of her five-year-old baby brother looking up at her at the end of a hard day in the field and asking, "Joycelyn, have we picked enough cotton? Do we have enough for you to go to school?"

Building homemade buses was a way for the community to improvise in the absence of resources, but building and maintaining a separate school system in the Jim Crow South was the quintessential act of improvisation. When the system wanted and expected the school and its teachers to provide a vocational education, the teachers did this and more. They taught the classics, higher-level math, and whatever they thought was part of what it meant to be educated for first-class citizenship. When the local school system expected the school and its teachers to teach the standard curriculum, to pass on the dominant narrative, the teachers did this and more. They taught about the history, culture, accomplishments, and struggles of African Americans. As Elders notes,

> Negro history was part of the same lesson. Everybody in school studied that. We talked about George Washington Carver and Booker T. Washington. We read Carter G. Woodson, the father of Negro history, who said if you control a man's mind, you control his actions, that we were programmed to think about ourselves the way the white world told us, but now it was time to control our own minds for ourselves. Frederick Douglass was there, and Charles Richard Drew, the great Black surgeon, and of course Sojourner Truth and Harriet Tubman. Our teachers taught us that black people were people of great courage and accomplishment, that they could raise themselves up. (54)

In other words, Elders and the students in her school were intentionally given counternarratives about themselves, about African Americans. Considering the reference to Douglass as an object of study, it is highly possible that Elders and the other students read Douglass's actual words about the relationship of literacy and learning to freedom. When the authorities expected the school to function as a broken-down, demoralized institution, the teachers, principal, and community made it into an institution of great pride for the entire community.

In this narrative, as in other narratives and historical accounts, Elders talks about how important graduation day was. It was a celebratory event for the entire community, even if there were only a few graduates. The graduates didn't just make their individual families proud; they made the community proud. Each graduate, and his or her narrative, was a living embodiment of the African-American philosophy of education.

Gwendolyn Parker

If Joycelyn Elders's narrative is the archetypal Black southern rural narrative, Gwendolyn Parker's memoir, *Trespassing: My Sojourn in the Halls of Privilege,* gives us a rare look into a life not usually associated with Black life in the segregated South. Parker's narrative chronicles her early years in an upper-middle-class family in the segregated South (Durham, North Carolina), her father's decision to move the family up north in search of greater opportunities for his children, and Gwendolyn's attempts to make sense of the challenges and opportunities of these environments, from elementary school to her work as a middle manager at American Express. Whatever class designation one chooses to assign to Parker's family, it is clear that her family was part of Durham's black elite—indeed the country's Black elite. Parker describes herself in the following manner. "I hailed from a small southern town once described as the home of the black middle class, was the daughter of a pharmacist and a teacher, granddaughter to a banker and a businessman, great granddaughter of a doctor who built one of the largest black-owned businesses" (Parker 1997, 2).

The contrast between the lives of Elders and Parker is stark. Elders was the daughter of sharecroppers, the daughter of a man who spent most of his time working in the field, the daughter of a woman who, while raising eight children, did the same, the daughter of a man who in whatever time he could carve out hunted raccoons so he could sell the skins for cash, eventually buying eighty acres of land and freeing the family from sharecropping.

Parker was the great-granddaughter of a man who built what was considered, when she was growing up, one of the largest Black businesses in the country, a man who had the distinction of having completed medical school at twenty-three, having received the second-highest score in the state on the medical boards. She was the great-granddaughter of a man who helped found and maintain critical Black institutions, a hospital, a college, and a library. While Elders worked hard in school, as if her life depended on it, she never thought much about going to college and having a career. For Parker, college and a career were givens. Elders grew up in a small rural community; Parker in a thriving city. They were of different generations—Elders of the pre–civil rights generation, Parker of the civil rights generation. And yet, despite these difference, their immediate and extended families deliberately passed on to them the African-American philosophy of schooling: education for freedom, for racial uplift, for leadership and citizenship.

For Parker, the first and possibly the most powerful lessons she learned about the meaning of education were concretized in the use to which individuals on both sides of her family put their education. They used their education to build, maintain, support, and work in and on behalf of institutions critical to the well-being of the African-American community. Her father, his brother, and her paternal great aunt all owned and operated pharmacies in the Black community. Her mother taught at the local Black college that Parker's maternal great-grandfather had helped to found. Her paternal grandmother was for many years president of the local NAACP, founded the church of which she was a member, and established the first youth chapter of the NAACP in the country. According to Parker, there was never a time in her life when she could not recite every detail of the history and accomplishments of her family, including the temperament, personality, and character of those who had passed away. As is often the case in African-American communities, her deceased relatives were talked about as if they were still alive. In the passing on of these narratives about her family, Parker learned that "whatever deeds that were accomplished, it was the meaning of these deeds that mattered: progress for the race, being the first, opening doors for those who will come behind, making our people proud." She also learned that for her great-grandfather "North Carolina Mutual was not simply a place to make money, but an institution charged with the betterment and uplift of a people." For Parker, "this heritage belonged to everyone who lived in Durham, but [she] was made to know that it had special meaning to her." These narratives were part of the oral tradition of the community, and as such they were used to motivate, to forge identity, to lay out what is possible, and to communicate the importance of education.

Indeed the use Parker's family made of their education was an ever-present location for Parker to imbibe the African Americans' philosophy of education. But it was her paternal grandmother who would convey the most direct messages about the meaning of schooling and learning, lessons that would serve Parker well once she moved to the North and found her intellectual ability routinely challenged.

In her everyday discourse, Grandmother Parker would often make special reference to those children in the community whom she considered smart, calling them "smart as a whip" or as "smart as they come." She took delight in telling stories about how smart Gwendolyn's father, her son, was, and even more delight in telling folk that "Gwenie Mac was smart, just as smart, maybe smarter" than he was

(25). This comment was usually followed by stories about how early Gwendolyn learned to talk in full sentences and to read, and about how well she was doing in school. The everyday act of telling stories about those who were smart and extolling them was very much a part of the discourse of people in my home community of Birmingham, Alabama, and of Black people throughout the South. For Grandmother Parker, "Smart was the best, the absolutely best you could be." Grandmother Parker was even more direct in her assessment of the function and meaning of learning and education. From Grandmother Parker, Gwendolyn learned that "intelligence is a weapon, a sharp, infinitely useful instrument, good for dealing with anyone, but especially with white folk, who, as she put it, never expected colored people to have any brains" (25).

If, in Parker's experience in the segregated South, being smart was an achievement to be aspired to, heralded, told stories about, and pursued, a term easily and readily applied to Black people regardless of their social class, in the North she would soon learn that Black people could be smart only by way of exception. This understanding would be expressed in the ideology of her teachers and institutionalized in the school's policies and practices. Thus Parker's narrative not only contains the African-American philosophy of schooling but also provides a dramatic example of how it is that Black came to be viewed as the antithesis of "being smart," and how "doing well in school" and "being smart" came to be associated with being and acting white.

Parker's narrative, like almost all other African-American narratives, provides its own versions of the dilemma of achievement experienced by Gwendolyn Parker and her family in the integrated North. The first experience occurs when Gwendolyn's father attempts to register her and her brothers for class in their new school, only to be told that they would have to be put back a class. The principal explained, "We find that it helps Southern Negro students to catch up." Gwendolyn's father responds to this impending decision by asking the principal if he had looked at his children's grades. Clearly, the principal had made the assumption that no matter how good their grades were, they were not ready for the grade they had been in in the South. Parker's father refused to back down, saying, "If they can't keep up, then you can put them back. I want them in with their class." This interaction would prefigure the story of Gwendolyn and her brothers' lives in this school, as her parents would continually have to bully the school system so that they could be in their right class, and later that they be allowed to be among the few Blacks enrolled in the advanced classes.

Predictably this first interaction enraged her parents. That evening, as her father recounted the details of his encounter with the principal, telling the story over and over again, their anger boiled over, and seemed to get more intense with each retelling. Parker recalls this episode:

> Whatever the principal had let loose, it now seemed to encompass so much more than him. I had always connected my parents' anger to something personal—something I or my brother had done, or something that made them mad at each other. This anger was different. It crashed about the room, free floating, huge, with a target that I couldn't see. And it didn't dissipate, but seemed to gather momentum as the evening went on. By the time my Uncle Eddie came home, the tale had been retold a dozen times, and he too joined in the anger. It felt to me like an anger that was decades, maybe a lifetime old. (36)

Parker was right; her parents were reacting to something that was old, ancient—the belief in Black intellectual inferiority.

This was a critical event for Parker's parents, one that captured the essence of what their fight for their children's education in the integrated North would be. If in the South the struggle was for equal facilities, equal pay for teachers, classroom buildings, a local high school, and materials, in the North the struggle would be against the assumption—no, the ideology—of Black children as intellectually inferior, and against school assignments, assessments, and interactions based on this ideology.

The incident that was a watershed for Gwendolyn, and one that fundamentally shaped how she would come to view educational work in the integrated North, involved an interaction with her white male English teacher, Mr. Bollen. Mr. Bollen was for Gwendolyn what Mr. Ostrowski was for Malcolm X. But unlike Malcolm, buffered by her large and ever-present extended family and their robust philosophy of education, she would not get derailed in her academic pursuits. She would explicitly call upon and use the African-American philosophy of learning as a counternarrative, to resist conclusions that Mr. Bollen and other teachers would make about her intellectual competence.

The incident began when Mr. Bollen gave the class a poetry-writing assignment. Gwendolyn loved to write, and from the time the assignment was given until it was due, she worked on it continually. Consider her words about the assignment and the eagerness with which she approached it:

> I had had many chances to show off my love of words in essays and on tests, but this was the first time in my new school I had been told to write a poem. For me, writing poetry had always been a secret pleasure. I had been writing poems for years, my first a few words on a napkin when I was five. I was so excited about the assignment I could hardly wait to get home and begin. I worked hard on my poem from the day it was assigned until the night before it was due. I was proud of the results, the poem rhymed in all the right places. I had struggled to make it about something on the surface and about something below the surface, as well as the two connected. (48)

The day finally came for Mr. Bollen to pass back the class papers. Another girl in the class, a white girl, who was Gwendolyn's best friend and who, like her, was one of the best students in the class, went up to get her paper. She returned to her seat with a smile on her face, for Parker an indication that she had received a good grade on this assignment. Gwendolyn Parker's name was finally called and she anxiously went up to get her paper. Gwendolyn could not believe the grade that she saw. Her grade was a C-minus, "which to her was as bad as failure." With tears in her eyes, she struggled to tell her teacher "this can't be right." Parker's description of her teacher's reaction is chilling, and unfortunately all too familiar to African-American youth:

> He stared at me as if he regretted my birth. It was a look filled with contempt and with anger. "There is no way that you could have written this poem," he said. "I searched all weekend, looking for where you may have copied it from. . . . If I'd been able to find out where you plagiarized it from, I would have given you an F. But since I couldn't find it, you are lucky I gave you a C–." (49)

Stunned, feeling as if the wind had been knocked out of her, Gwendolyn was self-possessed enough to say, "But I wrote it, I didn't copy it. I would never do that." Again Parker describes Mr. Bollen's stance toward her: "He looked at me again, with an expression so disdainful that it made me mute and invisible and impossibly small. Mr.

Bollen was certain that I couldn't have written that poem because it was too good and a Negro couldn't possibly write that well" (50, 51).

This was a critical event for Parker. It was not only devastating, but from that point on she allowed herself to see the many daily acts of discrimination that she had rationalized away. She now saw the teachers who "didn't call on her because they didn't expect her to have the answer, and when they learned she did, ignored her because they didn't want her to." She also allowed herself to remember that she didn't get the smiles or nods of approval that other children did when she gave a correct answer. She learned that her teachers had thought that she did well on tests because she copied from the paper of her best friend, and did well in math because her mother, a math teacher, did her work for her. But she also decided that if her teachers thought that a Black person couldn't be smart in her own right, she would show them otherwise. She studied with a mission, not only to learn but to disprove their assumptions about Black intellectual capacity.

On far too many occasions I have heard Black and white educators and scholars make the claim that Black students see doing well in school as white, assuming that the origin of this belief is Black peer culture. I have also heard the honest queries of African-American adults who were raised in the South and who remember the reverence for intellectual achievement, the special status attached to being smart, to knowing a lot, scratch their heads and ask, "how did it happen that what was so valued by us throughout our history and in our immediate past has become associated with being white?" Parker's narrative provides a partial answer. It is clear that in the minds of Parker's teachers being Black was not compatible with being smart. The narrative also makes it clear that in Parker's school this ideology had been institutionalized in policies and practices and also had been grudgingly accepted by the Black children in the school who were not part of that small group of children of educated parents who struggled to make their children the exception to the rule, to the ideology.

Almost as soon as Parker started at her new school, a group of Black girls began to pick on her, seemingly for no reason. None of these girls were in her class, the class for smart children, the class that her parents had fought to get her in. The group of Black girls teased her, called her names, tried to start a fight. In the same breath they called her, "Ms. Smarty Pant, Ms. Stuck Up, and Ms. No Butt." It is ironic that in their taunts they put what would have been, from a southern Black perspective, the ultimate insult in terms of physical appearance, "Not having a butt," on the same level with "thinking you are smart." And thus, even if it can be empirically demonstrated that Black youth see doing well in school as a white characteristic, the question that must be asked is, "What are the institutional formations and ideologies of teachers and schools that construct and reproduce these beliefs about schooling?" For Black parents and educators who still believe that it is good to be smart, to achieve, the question is, "How can African Americans' historic beliefs about being smart and achieving in school be passed on, considering the contemporary post–civil rights manifestations of the ideology of African-American intellectual inferiority in school?" I will return to these questions in part 3 of this essay.

Don L. Lee

In the sixties we knew him as Don L. Lee. Now he goes by the name of Haki Madhubuti, the author of *Don't Cry, Scream; Think Black;* and other collections of poetry. He was the poet of the sixties and seventies that you would travel miles to hear. His readings were standing-room-only events. We loved him while our parents and other adults worried about him. Eventually he would found and maintain for thirty years an independent school and a publishing house in Chicago, Illinois.

In the narrative of Joycelyn Elders we hear and feel the presence of her large extended family, her ever-present community, the children she walked to school with every day, the Saturday baseball games that her father played in, the community picnics that occurred like clockwork every Sunday after church. In contrast, in an interview with Cornel West, Haki focuses on his mother alone as the early critical influence in his life. In his later life he would be influenced by Black educators who had founded institutions and lived and worked in the Black community.

Haki doesn't sugarcoat the fact that his life was hard. He says,

> I grew up in a very impoverished community. Never having enough food, never having enough. I mean, I lived in a house where the lights would be off one day and on the next. You understand, it was difficult.

My mother basically ended up being committed by the system. Became
an addict, an alcoholic, and OD'd at the age of thirty-five. (West 1997,
164)

By age sixteen, Haki was on his own. What is powerful is that in
the midst of his mother's struggle with poverty and addiction, she had
the wherewithal to attempt to pass on to him his people's and her beliefs about education, her belief in the liberating and transforming
power of education. Haki recalls how his mother told him to go to the
library to check out *Black Boy* by Richard Wright so that he could read
it. In his interview with Cornel West, Haki admits that he was
ashamed to go to the white library and check out a Black book. Con-
sequently, he initially refused to comply with his mother's request.
But she persisted. He then went back to the library and found the
book. Putting it up against his chest so that nobody could see what the
title of the book was, he went to a section of the library where there
were no other people. He recalls how he then sat down and read and
read and read. The book captivated him. He checked the book out of
the library and went home and stayed up all night reading it. Reflecting on this experience, Haki says, "The next day I was not necessarily a different boy, but I began to see the world differently." In *Black
Boy*, Richard Wright recounts how important reading was to him, but
also how dangerous the whites he encountered thought it was. Upon
being discovered reading works by H. L. Mencken while working at a
factory, Wright's coworkers warned him that such writings were dangerous for a Negro to read, which further motivated Wright to read.
While Haki was on his way to basic training for the military, he encountered the same hostile reaction to his passion for reading.

In this group of recruits, all were white except Haki and two other
Black men. Haki was reading Paul Robeson's *Here I Stand*. The drill
sergeant snatched the book from his hand and said, "What your Negro mind doing reading this Black Communist?" He proceeded to
tear the book up, giving a page to each recruit and telling them to use
it for toilet paper. This incident profoundly affected Haki, and according to him, set him on a course for his life.

After this happened, it became clear that I needed to study with a mission.
And the mission was to become a self-informed person of African de-

scent. . . . If indeed the ideas in Paul Robeson's book . . . scared this man
so much that he would destroy it, then ideas were very powerful. (West
1997, 168)

These observations are hauntingly similar to Frederick Douglass's
comments on the intensity with which his master forbade his wife
from teaching him to read, and on the meaning of reading that
emerged from this prohibition.

Ben Carson

Like Haki, Ben Carson was raised by a single mother. His mother also
struggled with demons. For her it was mental illness, not drugs. In his
autobiography, Carson recalls that on at least two occasions his
mother had herself checked into a mental hospital. During one of
these times, he and his brother lived with a neighbor; during the
other, with family members. His mother was one of twenty children.
She married a man thirteen years her senior. She had only a third
grade education. In *Gifted Hands,* Ben narrates his path toward academic excellence and tells us of the singular and powerful role his
mother played in this journey.

Ben describes himself as the worst student in his class. As a matter
of fact, he recalls the embarrassment he often felt when, in his predominantly white classroom, the math papers were passed back.
When his name was called, and his weekly math test was returned, he
invariably had the worst score in the class. Not only was he embar-
rassed, but the other children in class made fun of him.

When he was in the fifth grade, his mother determined that he
and his brother would achieve in school. She had a two-pronged approach. First she would regularly tell them that they were smart and
how important reading was. Second, she reorganized their home lives
so that they could concentrate on schooling and so that reading could
become central. According to Carson, his mother would constantly
tell her sons, "I've got two smart boys, two mighty smart boys" (Carson and Murphey 1990, 34).

She also told them again and again, day in and day out, "If you can
read, honey, you can learn just about anything you want." Because
Ben was doing so badly in math, she first insisted that he learn his mul-

tiplication tables. After work, she drilled him. Ben was amazed that his math performance went from the bottom of the class to the top. Then his mother decided that the boys could watch only three hours of television a week and would visit the library regularly and read two books a week. They had to report to her on these books at the end of each week.

What is important is that Ben's mother not only passed on to her children a belief that they were smart and a belief in the power of reading, but she also put in place a set of practices that would give reality to this belief system. According to Ben, "My mother had such a faith in us, we didn't dare fail. Her unbounded confidence nudged me into starting to believe in myself." Almost daily, Ben Carson's mother said to him, "Benny you can do anything you set yourself to do" (Carson and Murphey, 37).

Septima Clark

Septima Clark was born in Charleston, South Carolina, to a washer-woman and a formerly enslaved man, two years before the close of the nineteenth century. In *Ready from Within: Septima Clark and the Civil Rights Movement,* Septima recounts the story of her life to Cynthia Stokes, a white woman. And as acknowledged by the writer, the narrative is necessarily filtered and informed by this relationship. Notwithstanding, the theme of literacy for freedom and citizenship figures centrally in this memoir. But this is not surprising when you consider the role that Septima played in the development of Citizenship Schools and the relationship of these schools to the Civil Rights movement and the struggle for the vote.

After having completed her education at the Avery Institute, Septima began her young adult life as a teacher in the Charleston, South Carolina, school system. Septima describes herself as the kind of person who from a very early age was willing to stand up to the unjust practices in the South. Her refusal to hide her membership in or resign from the NAACP resulted in her being fired from her job as a teacher, since it was against the law for city and state employees to be members of the NAACP. She went against established mores, the violation of which could have had serious consequences, and met with and engaged in social interactions with white people in her home and in the home of Judge Waring, the white judge who ruled all-white primaries in the South unconstitutional.

The theme of literacy for freedom and freedom for literacy is present throughout *Ready from Within*. It is captured most vividly in Septima's description of the role Esau Jenkins played in the development of the first Citizenship School, and in Septima's description of the role that she herself played in the development of the Citizenship Schools. Further, the philosophy of education, freedom for literacy and literacy for freedom, is explicitly expressed in Septima Clark's 1961 article, "Literacy Is Liberation," published in *Freedomways* in 1961. In this article Septima describes the many accomplishments of the Citizenship School movement, specifically the ways in which Citizenship Schools all over the South had motivated Black people to take control of their lives, to struggle for their freedoms. Throughout the article, as she discusses accomplishments of the Citizenship Schools, she includes the refrain "Literacy is liberation."

About two years after Septima was fired from her teaching job in Charleston, she became director of workshops for the Highlander Folk School in Tennessee. The Highlander Folk School was one of the few places in the South where Black and white people could come together to discuss their common and distinct oppression and prepare themselves to go back to their home communities to work on the local level to better their lives. Black and white people from the North who were committed to supporting this work also attended these sessions. The director of the Highlander Folk School was Myles Horton. In her narrative, Septima describes the intense conversations, more accurately described as disagreements, she had with Myles about how to approach Black voter registration in the South. According to Septima, Myles thought that all you needed to do was to go into a community, talk to people, and organize them to go down and register to vote. He did not know about the registration laws and specific literacy requirements for registering to vote for the different states. Septima recalls how she sent for copies of the registration laws for the southern states, laws that according to her Myles had never read. Eventually Myles relented, as he came to understand why Septima had insisted that literacy training had to be a critical element of any voter registration organizing effort. This was the conceptual origin of the Citizenship

School movement. It would appear that Septima's unique contribution to the development of the Citizenship School was the systematic linking of literacy training to voter registration organizing. While Septima was able to change Myles's perspective, she noted that she changed as well. She emerged from this dispute with Myles being better able to stand up to and disagree with a white person.

Septima Clark's relationship with Esau Jenkins of St. John's Island was the context out of which the first Citizenship School developed on St. John's Island. It was Septima who, after much cajoling, persuaded Esau to attend workshops at Highlander School. Esau Jenkins was a small farmer, the father of eight children, who supplemented his income by operating a bus service for the children and workers in his community. For many years, even before he began to attend workshops at the Highlander School, Esau had been involved in efforts to improve the conditions of the lives of Black people on St. John's Island. Esau had run for school committee and lost the election even though all of the Black people on the island who were registered had voted for him. The problem was that voter registration in South Carolina, as in many southern states, had a literacy requirement. Although it is not mentioned in the narrative, one can imagine that after Esau lost the election, there were many conversations on the island about how important it was for Blacks to be registered if they were going to exercise their citizenship rights, and given the voter registration requirements, the importance of becoming literate. What we *are* told is that one day when Esau was transporting Black workers to Charleston, a woman stepped in and offered to do her part, probably offering a response to the postelection conversations that had occurred throughout the island. She said,

> I don't have much schooling, Esau. . . . I wasn't even able to get though the third grade. But I would like to be somebody. I'd like to hold my head up with other people; I'd like to be able to vote. Esau, If you'll help me a little when you have the time, I'll be glad to learn the laws and get qualified to vote. If I do, I promise you I'll register and I'll vote. (Clark 1990, 46)

Esau had South Carolina's voter registration laws and requirements typed up, and he passed out copies of them to the people who rode on his bus. When he was transporting his passengers, before the

bus left taking them to work, and before people assembled for their return home, he would help people read, understand, and interpret the
laws and the U.S. Constitution. Indeed, the woman who initially
asked for his help managed to prepare herself so that she was able to
register and vote. Because she had such a wonderful memory, she was
able to memorize the Constitution. While memorizing and being
able to interpret the Constitution had been enough to enable her to
register to vote, that wasn't enough for her. She wanted to be fully literate. Again she went to Esau for help, asking if there was a school
where she could work on reading and writing. There was none. Esau
then went about the business of trying to find a place where he could
open a school that would be devoted to systematically improving the
literacy skills of the adults on the island and preparing them to register
to vote. He thought about the predictable places—churches and
schools—but these were not available, because of Black people's fear
of reprisals from white people. The minister he approached about the
use of his church was afraid that if he were to allow Esau to use his
church for literacy and voter registration classes, the authorities would
find out and his wife would lose her job as a teacher. The school principal he approached was also afraid. Because of Esau's association with
the Highlander School and through the intercession of Septima
Clark, Esau was able to secure a loan from the Highlander School to
purchase a building that could be used as a school. The front part of
the building was made into a store that was operated by the Progressive Association, a self-help organization of which Esau was a member; the two rooms in the back were to be used for teaching. Of the
plan for the building, Septima says, "We planned the grocery store to
fool white people. We didn't want them to know that we had a school
back there. . . . We didn't have windows back there at that time, so
white people couldn't peep in. That's the way we planned it" (47).

This one school would soon expand to five schools on other islands. By the spring of 1961, working as director of teacher training
for the Highlander Folk School, Septima had trained eighty-two
teachers who were holding classes in Alabama, Georgia, South Carolina, and Tennessee. Septima traveled throughout the South, visiting
teachers who were operating Citizenship Schools and recruiting individuals to be trained as Citizenship School teachers. She recruited
individuals who were well respected in their home communities,

who could read well orally, and who could write legibly in cursive. She was particularly interested in individuals who were good listeners, as one of the first tasks of the teacher was to find out what people wanted to know. Besides wanting to have enough knowledge to enable them to register to vote, Black people throughout the South sometimes wanted to know about how the local government worked, or how to fill out a money order or write a check. In other words, they often wanted to know how to secure their citizenship, to liberate themselves, and to take control of their lives.

Eventually, because of harassment of the Highlander School by local authorities and the threat of its closure, the sponsoring agency for the Citizenship Schools was transferred from the Highlander School to the Southern Christian Leadership Conference and located in the Dorcester Center in MacIntosh, Georgia. Between 1957 and 1970, over eight hundred Citizenship Schools were in operation. Here is Septima's assessment of the impact of the Citizenship Schools:

> In 1964 there were 195 going at one time. They were in people's kitchens, in beauty parlors, and under trees in the summer time. I went all over the south visiting three citizenship schools in one day, checking to be sure they weren't using textbooks, but were teaching people to read those election laws and to write their names in cursive. One time I heard Andy Young say that these citizenship schools were the base on which the whole civil rights movement was built. And that's probably very much true. (69–70)

In reflecting on the theme of literacy for freedom and citizenship, several points are in order. When the woman approaches Esau for his help in teaching her to read, she says she wants to read so she can be somebody. This is the language that is used is other narratives of the Jim Crow era, including that of Joycelyn Elders, whose mother and grandmother both urged her to get an education so she could be somebody. Reading, being literate, getting an education in the Black collective consciousness are all acts that affirm one as a human, as a person of worth, as somebody, as a freeman or woman, one who is the opposite of a slave.

In the fifties and sixties, it was not against the law to read, or to teach others to read or write, but the literacy requirements for registering to vote that were in effect throughout the South most certainly further solidified in the African-American consciousness the historic philosophy of education, freedom for literacy and literacy for freedom. The registration laws legally encoded the notion that literacy was a requirement for citizenship and freedom.

As late as the early sixties, in the context of the Citizenship School movement and voter registration organization, pursuing literacy was still seen as a subversive act that carried punitive consequences. It had to be done with some secrecy. In these instances, as in the time of slavery, African Americans improvised, found spaces in the interstices of life to become literate and to help others become literate. While Blacks were no longer huddled in the woods, they were on St. John's Island having literacy classes in a secret back room with no windows. In the context of the Citizenship Schools, literacy was used to overcome one of the legally constructed barriers to voting, but literacy classes were also used to help people secure other freedoms, whether that meant learning about one's local government or learning how to write one's name in cursive so that one could write checks.

Maya Angelou

The graduation scene described in Maya Angelou's autobiographical narrative *I Know Why the Caged Bird Sings* asks and answers the question, Why literacy? This sequence embodies the dilemma of achievement for African Americans living in the segregated South, a people whose school and community were organized to affirm their humanity, their racial, cultural, and national identities, and to buffer them from ideologies, policies, and practices that would devalue and denigrate them.

The entire school community took on an air of celebration as Maya and her classmates prepared for graduation. All its members were involved in the preparations—building sets and preparing speeches, dramatic readings, and songs. The graduation was a celebration not only for the graduates and the families of the children attending the school, but for the entire community. While each student's achievements were noted with great fanfare, the graduation itself, and the graduation of each student, was a communal event, an accomplishment for the African-American community of Stamps, Arkansas.

Against the backdrop of this excitement and celebratory atmosphere, the inequalities represented in the physical conditions of the Black county school and the white county school loomed large. Maya reflects on the difference:

> Unlike the white high school, Lafayette County Training School distinguished itself by having neither lawn nor hedges, nor tennis court, nor climbing ivy. Its two buildings (main classrooms, the grade school, and home economics) were set on a dirt hill with no fence to limit either its boundaries, or those of the bordering farms. There was a large expanse to the left of the school, which was used alternately as a baseball diamond or basketball court. Rusty hoops on the swaying poles represented the permanent recreational equipment, although bats and balls could be borrowed from the P. E. teachers, if the borrower was qualified, and if the diamond wasn't occupied. (Angelou 1969, 151)

Despite these inequalities, Maya and her classmates were committed to academic achievement. They diligently studied Black poets and Black history, and they were also steeped in the so-called classics, given an education usually reserved for those considered "first-class citizens" by the larger society. However, only a small number of the students graduating from the high school would attend college, and many of them would attend a college with an ostensibly vocational curriculum, suggesting that they were being prepared to reproduce their social position in the larger society. The dilemma of achievement for African Americans is concretized in the very nature of separate and unequal education.

Graduation day was one of particular excitement for Maya's family and friends. Maya's grandmother had bought her a watch as a graduation present. Her brother Bailey had given her a bound leather copy of the works of Edgar Allen Poe. Maya's grandmother owned a store, and nearly every one of her customers had given Maya a gift: "a nickel, maybe a dime, with the instruction 'keep on moving to higher ground' or some other encouragement." Maya's grandmother posted a sign on her store announcing the importance of the day. It read, "Closed—graduation."

The graduation began with the traditional opening sequence for ceremonies in the Black community: the singing of the national anthem, the Pledge of Allegiance, and the singing of the Black National Anthem. This ceremony was interrupted after the Pledge of Allegiance by two white men, representatives from the county. The graduates and other members of the audience were motioned by the principal to be seated.

One of the white men made his way to the podium, allegedly to bring greetings and congratulations to the graduates. With these greetings, he let those in attendance know, in no uncertain terms, that contrary to what they might imagine, they were not being educated for first-class citizenship, for freedom. Maya recalls the white man's message to the graduates, to their families and to the Stamps community:

> He told us of the wonderful changes we children in Stamps had in store. The Central School (naturally, the white school was "central") had already been granted improvements that would be used in the fall. A well-known artist was coming from Little Rock to teach art to them. They were going to have the newest microscopes and chemistry equipment for their laboratory. . . .
>
> He said that he had pointed out to people at a very high level that one of the first-line halfback tacklers at Arkansas Agricultural and Mechanical College had graduated from Lafayette County Training School. . . .
>
> He went on to praise us. He went on to say how he had bragged "one of the best basketball players sank his first ball right here at Lafayette County Training School." . . .
>
> The white kids were going to have a chance to be the Galileos and Madame Curies and Edisons and Gauguins, and our boys (the girls weren't even in on it) would try to be Jessie Owenses and Joe Lewises. (151–52)

Maya's words revealed the absurdity of this graduation event. The existential dilemma about the meaning of academic achievement for African Americans was "thrown in the faces" of the graduates and their community. The magic evaporated, the spirit of celebration and excitement dissipated. Those in attendance came face-to-face with their history as a despised and degraded people, with their identity as a racially and historically oppressed people:

Graduation, the hush-hush magic time of thrills and gifts and congratulations and diplomas, was finished for me before my name was called. The
accomplishment was nothing. The meticulous maps drawn in three
colors of ink, learning and spelling decasyllabic words, memorizing the
whole of "The Rape of Lucrece"—it was for nothing. Donleavy [the
white speaker] had exposed us. . . .

We were maids and farmers, handymen and washerwomen, and anything higher that we aspired to was farcical and presumptuous. (152)

Maya writes that the ugliness that followed these remarks was palpable, that it refused to leave, even after the white men who had
"hand-delivered" it left as abruptly as they had entered. Neither the
singing of "Onward Christian Soldiers" nor the recitation of the
poem "Invictus" cleared the air. Maya allows us access to her thoughts
as the valedictorian began his speech, to her struggles with the absurdity of her community's commitment to academic achievement, to
literacy:

There was shuffling and rustling around me, then Henry Reed was giving his valedictory address, "To Be or Not to Be." Hadn't he heard the
white folks? We couldn't *be*, so the question was a waste of time. Henry's
voice came out clear and strong. I feared to look at him. Hadn't he got the
message? There was no "nobler in the mind" for Negroes, because the
world didn't think we had minds, and they let us know it. "Outrageous
fortune?" Now, that was a joke. When the ceremony was over, I had to
tell him to read some things, if I still cared. (152)

As soon as Henry Reed had completed his speech, he turned to
face the graduates on stage, leading them and the entire community in
singing the Black National Anthem, which had been omitted because
of the visit of the white folks from downtown.

Lift every voice and sing
Till earth and heaven ring
Ring with harmonies of liberty
Stony the road we rode
Bitter the chastening rod
Felt in the days when hope, unborn, had died
Yet with a steady beat
Have not our weary feet
Come to the place for which our fathers sighed? (Angelou 1969, 155)

The singing of the Black National Anthem by the entire community, and the historic meaning of this ritual, reminded the community of the answer to the question, Why literacy? The unbowed display of an individual, followed by the collective gesture together turned the community back to a focus on education as an act of freedom, as an act of resistance, as a political and communal act.

After singing the Black National Anthem, Maya recalls that the community was "on top again. . . . The depths had been icy and dark, but now bright sun spoke to our souls. I was no longer simply a member of the proud graduating class of 1940; I was a proud member of the wonderful, beautiful Negro race" (156). This graduation sequence reflects the institutionalization of the African-American philosophy of schooling, freedom for literacy and literacy for freedom, and its capacity to develop and sustain the desire to achieve in a historically oppressed group.

REFLECTIONS ON THE NARRATIVES

What lessons emerge from our reading of the narratives? How can these lessons inform the contemporary conversation about African-American school achievement?

Academic achievement, doing well in school, and pursuing learning, in all of these narratives, is always accomplished in the face of considerable constraints, whether the impoverished condition of the school, the absence of a local high school, laws that made it a crime to teach slaves to read and write, or a teacher's or school's ideology of African-American intellectual inferiority. These constraints were tied to the social identity and the political location of African Americans *as* African Americans.

The pursuit of education as described in the narratives is not casual. It is seen and presented as intense, persistent, and supported and fueled by an explicit and continually articulated belief system. This explicit, and continually articulated belief system functions as a counternarrative, one that stands in opposition to the dominant society's notions about the intellectual capacity of African Americans, the role of learning in their lives, the meaning and purpose of school, and the power of their intellect.

The authors use metaphors to capture the embeddedness and the all-embracing nature of their or their community's beliefs about education. These beliefs were ground up and served as grits, communicated with the regularity of a mother's prayers, like a drumbeat, a mission.

Many of the narratives place in the foreground the set of behaviors, the routines and practices, that express in the real world the individuals' and their families' commitment to learning—from Douglass, who took his spelling book with him so that whenever he had time he could practice his reading; to Malcolm, who read whenever he had time, even late at night; to Carson, who at his mother's insistence read every night.

The narratives we have cited have a discursive function and as such are powerfully implicated in the identity formation of African Americans as learners and intellectual beings. Not only are stories passed down from generation to generation about the meaning of literacy and the meaning of the denial of literacy, but these narratives show African Americans who they can become. As Dorothy Holland and others maintain, "Identities are the stories we tell ourselves and the world about who we are, and our attempt to act in accordance with these stories." For Elders, it was the story of Edith Folb, the first woman and the first Black person to graduate from the University of Arkansas Medical School, told at Philander-Smith College's weekly chapel service, that allowed her to see herself as a doctor. It was the story of Douglass's and other slaves' pursuit of literacy "in danger and darkness," passed on orally to Elders and almost certainly read by her in written narrative text, that motivated her to be committed to learning. It was the narrative of Richard Wright that figured centrally in Haki's redefinition of himself as a literate person. And it was the stories of her family and what they were willing to do with their education that framed the identity and possibilities for Gwendolyn Parker.

The philosophy of achievement that emerges from these narratives is predicated on, is responsive to, and exists in a dialectical relationship with the specific challenges African Americans faced in their pursuit of education and literacy. It is a philosophy that is predicated on and takes seriously the sociopolitical location of African Americans. For Africans in America, literacy laws were enacted to keep them as a people from voting, from exercising their citizenship rights. African-American teachers were paid less than white teachers, less was spent on African-American schools, and so on. There was a systematic denial and limiting of educational opportunity for African Americans precisely because they were African Americans. The philosophy of education that developed was informed by the particular ways in which literacy and education were implicated in the oppression of African Americans. It informed the role that education and schooling would assume in resistance and the struggle for freedom from the time of slavery to the Civil Rights era.

But what do all of these observations have to do with the current conversation about African-American school achievement? For what groups of African Americans, for what generations, is this philosophy of education still compelling? Among contemporary African-American youth, could this philosophy of education have the power to make academic achievement coincident with being African American? How would it be manifested, ritualized, represented in the post–Civil Rights era? Can it still play a role in the identity formation of African-American children? Could it play a central role in motivating contemporary African Americans to pursue education vigorously? If it is true that the media plays a central role in the construction of racial and gender identities, can a counternarrative about African Americans as intellectuals have sufficient power to contest the negative narratives about African Americans that are expressed in the media and encoded in the ideologies and practices of schools? What would it take for this historic philosophy of education to be systematically and intentionally passed on in families, community-based organizations, and schools? Under what conditions could it be passed on in a multiracial, multicultural school community?

And finally, how can this philosophy of achievement enter into dialogue with and be used to critique the explanatory models and their variations that have been used and continue to be used to discuss school performance of African Americans and other children of color? How would it be used in the development of a theory of achievement for African Americans at the beginning of the twentieth century?

PART TWO

COMPETING THEORIES OF
GROUP ACHIEVEMENT

In part 1 of this essay, we heard the voices of African Americans and reflected on how they developed a philosophy of education, which equated their social identity as a free people with the pursuit of literacy and learning. In this section, I will examine two theoretical frameworks that have been influential in academic circles and popular conversations that purport to explain and predict the school performance of racial minorities: the cultural difference and social mobility explanatory models. Even though when applied to African Americans, the initial focus of both of these models was on explaining school failure, I have chosen to discuss these models in my attempt to theorize African-American school success, because with both the focus is on social group identity rather than differences between and among individuals. As articulated earlier, I am contending that the task of achievement for African Americans is complicated, made distinctive, because of African Americans' social group identity. Analyzing these theories will allow me to identify insights, understandings, and problems that can inform the development of a theory of African-American achievement. Because scholars, educators, and especially teacher–educators routinely rely on these theories and variations of them in their explanations of the school performance of students of color and in the preparation of teachers to work with students of color, I am hopeful that this analysis will occasion a change in the way these theories are presented and discussed when applied to African Americans.

THE CULTURAL DIFFERENCE EXPLANATION
FOR SCHOOL PERFORMANCE

Cultural difference theorists argue that the disproportionate school failure of African Americans and other racial minorities can be attributed at best to a mismatch and at worst to a conflict between a student's home culture and the culture of the school. The assumption is that the culture of the school is the dominant culture, the culture of white mainstream America. Probably because language is so central to work in school and to social identity, much of the early work of cultural difference theorists was focused on language. As James Baldwin notes,

> Language is the most vivid and crucial key to identity. It reveals the private and connects one with, or divorces one from the larger, public, or communal identity. To open your mouth in England is (if I may use Black English) to put your business in the street. You have confessed your parent, your youth, your school, your salary, your self-esteem, and alas, your future. (Baldwin 1985, 650)

Since the early scholarly work on language conflict occurred when the country was in the midst of the Civil Rights movement and just beginning the struggle to desegregate its schools, all of which was cast primarily in black-white terms, almost all of the early work of cultural difference theorists focused on how the home language that Black children brought to school conflicted with the language of the dominant society, the language of the school. It is important to note that cultural difference theorists were at pains to distinguish their work from the earlier work of educators and cognitive psychologists who had unapologetically maintained either that Black language and culture were deficient or that Black children entered school with no language, or both.

William Labov (1972a, b) and others conducted research on Black English that established, contrary to the deficiency interpretations, that Black English was a distinct, systematic, rule-based language, capable of accommodating the full range of intellectual and cognitive tasks. This research did not, however, prevent teachers then or now from making judgments about the intellectual capacity of children based on their speech, or from correcting children's African-American-accented readings of texts, a translation that suggests receptive competence in edited American English and African-American language. After much discussion and debate, the considered opinion was that Black English was not in itself a barrier to the school performance of African-American students. It was problematic only in terms of what it represented for teachers and the reactions it elicited from them. It was problematic in light of the test specialists' failure to develop assessment instruments that could accurately and adequately distinguish between language disabilities and language differences. It was problematic to the extent that a teacher's knowledge base and attitudes did not equip him or her, in theory or in practice, to distinguish difference from deficiency.

In the early seventies, researchers were urged to shift the focus of their work on language. While the earlier conversation about Black language and its potential to be a barrier to the successful school performance of African-American children had focused on the language itself—its grammar, its sound system, its words—the new focus would be expanded to include how language was used in the classroom. Children, like adults, were thought to be members of speech communities, usually paralleling the major divisions in society, in terms of race, gender, class, and ethnicity—with different rules for asking questions, taking turns, getting the floor, expressing functional intent and emotions, exercising control, and so on. What happens when youth come to school from discourse communities that have different discourse rules, particularly for those speech acts that are central to classroom communication?

Now it is not hard for those of us who are from working-class or poor families, or who are members of a racial minority group, to identify with the reasonableness and emotional import of the cultural difference explanation for school performance. We know what it is like to have something to say in a class but not to be heard because of our accented English or communication style. We know what it is like to have judgments made about our intelligence because of our speech, to be silenced by our teachers or even by ourselves because of fear of not expressing ourselves in an acceptable manner. If we are African American, we have undoubtedly expressed our opinion strongly in a class, only to be accused of being angry, mad, or out of control.

Research studies were conducted that documented cultural conflict in the classroom, a mismatch between the rules of language use in the child's home and the rules of language use required for full participation in the classroom. With this research came the call for culturally responsive pedagogy, pedagogy based on knowledge of and sensitivity to the culturally learned communication styles that students of color brought to school. Let me point to several examples, one from research and two from practice, all of which have been used to illustrate the theorized cause and effect relationship frequently drawn between culturally responsive practice and improved school performance.

In a series of controlled experiments, Kathryn Au (1980) compared the results that followed when different methods of discussion were used with two different groups of Hawaiian children after they had read stories. One group used the standard Anglo mainstream method of turn-taking, where one person follows another; the other used "talk story," a traditional Hawaiian method of turn-taking, which permits overlapping talk and allows children to jump in and participate, not waiting until one child has finished talking. The use of talk story discussion following the reading lesson resulted in more enthusiastic participation by the children and increased reading comprehension as measured by a test administered immediately after the discussion.

Judith Richards (1993), a teacher in Cambridge, Massachusetts, recounts her experience in a third/fourth grade classroom of children of white and African-American professionals and working-class Haitian immigrants. When she structured a traditional math problem-solving activity, the children of professionals invariably took the lead. However, when she embedded the same type of math problem-solving activity in a traditional Haitian folk tale, the Haitian children took the lead.

It seems reasonable that culturally responsive pedagogy would positively affect learning. In both instances, the cognitive task facing children from cultures that were different from mainstream culture was simplified when they did not have to deal with both an unfamiliar speech event and instructional content. Further, one can imagine that using a familiar communication style could possibly reduce cultural dissonance, create a sense of membership, and symbolically affirm children who are members of racial minority groups (Erickson 1987).

A final case illustrates how culturally responsive teaching practices affect the academic performance of African-American children. In a collection of writings on the 1996 Ebonics debate (Perry and Delpit 1998), Carrie Secret, an elementary teacher, provides us with a robust description of culturally responsive pedagogy based on her use of Black language and communication style. The Ebonics debate emerged from the Black community's efforts to respond to the gap in school achievement in the Oakland, California, school district between African-American children on the one hand and white and Asian-American children on the other. The Prescott Elementary School, where Carrie Secret was teaching, was one of the few schools in the Oakland school district where African-American children were achieving (based on standardized test scores). And what was distinctive about this school was that all of its teachers had participated in an educational program where they had learned about Black language* and were committed to systematically having their knowledge of Black language and culture influence their teaching practices.

In the description of her practice, Carrie Secret includes the multiple ways she uses African-American language and culture in all aspects of her teaching. For Secret, helping African-American children acquire fluency in the standard code is not about helping them correct their home language. Rather, it is about helping them acquire fluency in another language. Using contrastive analysis with her students, she uses her knowledge of Black language to help her students understand how their home language differs systematically from edited American English. Sometimes this means helping her students hear differences in pronunciation that they don't automatically hear, and even overenunciating endings that they might routinely drop. In this regard, I am reminded of how, even today, it is difficult for me, having been born and reared in Birmingham, Alabama, to hear when I have produced the Black-inflected pronunciation of "ask." And if I don't consciously think about it, I will inevitably pronounce the word "ask" as "ax."

Carrie Secret describes how she routinely exposes her students to models of Black literary excellence, individuals who, in their writ-

---

*In the late-sixties conversation about African-American language, "Black English" was the term used to refer to the language African Americans spoke. More recently, in order to move away from a definition of African-American language as a dialect, some scholars have chosen to characterize the language of African Americans as either Black language or Ebonics.

ings—sometimes in the same text, and other times in different texts —write in both Black language and edited American English. In her practice, she affirms that these two modes of linguistic expression are not only not in contradiction with each other but ultimately compatible, and more to the point, evidence of literary excellence. She further asserts that the literature that is written by African Americans in Black language "just feels good" to her African-American students.

Drawing on the centrality of oral performance in the Black community, Secret uses the oral performance of literary texts, speeches, poems, and portions of essays to build community, create hope, inspire the children, and extend their vocabulary. This practice is reminiscent of the role and function of oral performance in the Black segregated schools. In 1896, Miles V. Lynk published *The Afro American School Speaker and Gems of Literature.* In the introduction he says, "If the colored youth of this country become imbued with these exalted ideas, no power on earth can prevent their rapid rise and keep them from occupying a position in line with that of the foremost races of the world." Similar collections of African-American oratory were published and used by Black teachers throughout the twentieth century—thus providing an answer to Joycelyn Elders's query as to why Black folk who attended segregated schools seemed to know and have performed the same texts.

Understanding the role of music in Black culture, Secret uses music—Black popular and classical music and European classical music—to help her students center and calm themselves, and to help them focus. Carrie Secret understands that what makes students powerful is not simply their acquisition of the standard code, but their fluency in content knowledge and their familiarity with many literatures and the language of many different disciplines. Perhaps most important, she does not see this broad knowledge as oppositional to the language and culture of African Americans. For in her classroom, she readily draws upon and uses the cultural characteristics that have been identified as central to African-American culture to ground her educational practice. She also creates multiple speech events in her classroom, events in which students are expected to practice speaking and presenting in edited American English. She frames these events as "formal locations," some of which are construed as formal locations or events within the Black community, and others as formal events in

society at large. For example, she sometimes asks her students to imagine that they are students at Spelman or Morehouse College and to
think about how they would be required to speak in these situations.
She also expects her students to speak in edited American English
when they have visitors and when they make reports to the class
on their group work. Using culturally responsive practices deeply
engages Secret's largely African-American student body, and they
achieve high levels.

Since the 1970s, when researchers were asked to shift the focus of
their work from the language itself to how language was used in the
classroom, the impact of cultural difference theory has been significant. It has been the basis for two high-profile cases on Black language.
It has resulted in rich descriptions of the culturally responsive teaching practices of Black and white teachers. It continues to generate
new and interesting research, such as the use of Haitian argumentation
style in teaching scientific reasoning, and the use of the African-
American speech act of signifying to teach literary analysis. More important, it has helped many teachers become attentive to and draw on
the cultural and linguistic practices of their students (Ballanger 1997;
Lee 1993; Ladson-Billings 1994; Delpit 1995; Conant 1996). Notwithstanding the significant contributions of the cultural difference
theory to research and teaching, by itself, it has limitations as an explanatory model for African-American school performance.

THE SOCIAL MOBILITY EXPLANATION
FOR SCHOOL PERFORMANCE

In the early 1980s John Ogbu emerged as the most influential critic
of the cultural difference theory. Ogbu (1983) criticized educational
anthropologists who conducted cultural mismatch studies for their
proliferation of microethnographies, which reduced culture to de-
contextualized practices. He argued for a conceptualization of culture
as "lived experiences," ecological and historical. Perhaps Ogbu's most
serious critique of cultural difference theory was his challenge of
its explanatory power: it might have offered an explanation for the
school failure of some minorities, but it did not explain variation in
school performance among racial minority groups. That is, it did
not explain why some groups whose cultures were different from the

mainstream, such as Asian Americans, did not experience disproportionate failure, but rather success. And further, even though in Carrie
Secret's description of her work with children at the Prescott Elementary School we have an example of culturally responsive practice that
is all-encompassing and that results in academic achievement for
African-American children, we also know of schools that are far from
culturally responsive (Catholic schools, military schools, and independent schools), where African-American children also achieve. Is
there an explanatory model for the school performance of African
Americans that would be able to explain achievement in these seemingly very different contexts?

Having examined achievement data for racial minorities in the
United States and in other countries, Ogbu argues that being a racial
minority and having a different culture does not in itself predict
school failure. He notes significant variation in school performance
among racial minorities in this country, and within racial groups in
different geographical contexts. For example, whereas African Americans, Native Americans, and Chicanos experience disproportionate
school failure in this country, Japanese Americans, Chinese Americans, and Filipinos do not. Further complicating the picture, Chinese
peasants and Burakumin (despised classes of ethnic Japanese) achieve
academically in this country but fail disproportionately in schools in
Hong Kong and Japan.

Ogbu's (1983) comparison of the achievement data of racial minorities, plus his ethnographic study of school achievement among
Chinese-American and African-American children in Stockton,
California, led him to conclude that being a member of a racial minority does not necessarily predict school performance. Rather, it is
the terms of the group's incorporation into the host society and the
group's social position in that society that predict and explain school
performance. On this basis, Ogbu develops an explanation for variation in the school performance of domestic minorities that is critically
informed by his categories of "immigrant minority" and "castelike
minority."

According to Ogbu, in a racially stratified society, all racial minorities experience social and economic discrimination and are the vic-
tims of racism, stereotyping, and a "glass ceiling." What distinguishes
immigrant and castelike minorities is the attitude with which they

face this treatment. Immigrant minorities come to this country voluntarily, usually seeking a better life. Accepting the white middle-class theory of achievement—if you work hard, you will get ahead —immigrant minorities view their problems as "more or less temporary," linked to their status as new immigrants. They do not compare their life and treatment in the host country with that of the white mainstream group, but with their peers in their country of origin. In the context of this comparison, their life here appears better. Further, as immigrants they retain the possibility of returning to their countries of origin.

Racially oppressed or castelike minorities, on the other hand, were brought into this country involuntarily, either through force, as in the case of African Americans, or by conquest, as with Native Americans and Mexicans in the Southwest. "Membership in a castelike group is permanent, ascribed at birth" (Ogbu 1983, 171). Over generations, castelike minorities have occupied the status of oppressed peoples, have been confined to low-level jobs, and have had little or no political power. Typically society has developed an ideology of racial inferiority to rationalize and explain their position. There is no homeland to which to return.

For castelike minorities, the point of comparison is the dominant group. If their life chances are less than or different from those of white Americans, they are not satisfied. According to Ogbu (1990, 65), "they wish they could get ahead through education and ability, but they know that they can't because of racial barriers which they interpret as part of their undeserved oppression." Moreover, whereas immigrant minorities tend to trust white Americans, castelike minorities do not. An African-American man interviewed by Janie Ward (1991,2), was asked, "If you were to create a racial survival kit, what would you put in it?" The man responded, "A set of eyes in the back of your head."

Notwithstanding their experience of discrimination, immigrant minorities vigorously embrace the dominant American ideology that hard work and education pay off and will lead to a better life. Castelike minorities, on the other hand, have lived here for generations, observing the lives of their parents and other members of their communities, and have come to believe that education does not necessarily lead to better jobs—for members of their group. While castelike minority parents articulate a strong belief in the importance of education for getting ahead and making it in this society, at the same time they communicate to their children an ambivalence about whether society will really reward them for their school achievement. This phenomenon has led to what Ogbu (1983, 1990) has called a lack of "effort optimism" (1990, 81) among the children of castelike minorities.

Ogbu is to be congratulated for locating at the center of his discussion of the school achievement of America's people of color their social history and political location in the society over time, and how these realities are necessarily related to effort optimism. In so doing, he calls attention to the role of individual and collective consciousness in school achievement and how that consciousness has been affected by the job market and the schooling experiences of African Americans in general, and their families and communities in particular. He questions how the social history of African Americans and their historic and contemporary relationships with the job market and schools have informed their philosophy of schooling, their folk theory of achievement. His struggle is to understand the psychology, motives, and intentionality of African Americans as they go to school. Although his methodology is promising, the conclusions he draws from his reading and understanding of the social history of African Americans are seriously flawed.

Ogbu maintains that African Americans' fight for equal educational opportunity has left them with a deep distrust for schools and school people. In his work with Signithia Fordham, he argues that African Americans have developed both an oppositional identity, "a sense of peoplehood in opposition to the social identity of white Americans because of the way white American treated them" (Fordham and Ogbu 1986) and an oppositional cultural framework that identifies certain activities, including doing well in school, as "white activities." As a consequence, individuals who choose to engage in white-identified activities risk being ostracized by the Black community. He further maintains that this cultural framework toward schooling resides not only in Black peer culture, but also in the African-American community as a whole. According to Ogbu, African Americans have not developed an academic tradition. Relying on Ogbu's misguided definition of African-American culture as purely oppositional, based on an ethnographic study of Capital High School in Washington, D.C., Fordham argues that the Black students at Capitol High School see doing well in school as "acting white." This is the scholarly origin of the popular claim that Black students see academic achievement as a white activity. A close reading of Fordham's work suggests that the evidence she presents could just as easily be marshaled to support the counterclaim that it was the culture and organization of Capital High School, rather that Black peer culture, that required Black students who would be achievers to distance themselves from Black culture and become white.

What is deeply problematic is Ogbu's reading, knowledge, and interpretation of African-American social and educational history and how it has influenced contemporary attitudes. There is simply no evidence to support the claim that African Americans historically developed a deep distrust of school and school people. Ogbu could not have made the assertion that African Americans have not developed an academic tradition if he had known of African Americans' epic historical struggle for literacy and educational opportunity, of the county graduations that drew thousands of spectators, about the amazing African-American literary tradition, about the 130-year history of Black literary societies, about the penny schools and native schools, and I could go on. The following comments of two leading historians, although not specifically directed at Ogbu, nonetheless offer their own powerful critiques of Ogbu's reading and understanding of Black educational history.

In the epilogue of *The Education of Blacks in the South, 1860–1935,* James Anderson observes:

> It is ironic that in time a body of historical and social science literature was built up which tended to interpret blacks' relatively lower levels of educational attainment in the twentieth century as the product of initial differences in attitude or cultural orientation toward learning and self improvement. . . . A careful examination of blacks' enduring beliefs in education and their historic struggles to acquire decent educational opportunities against almost overwhelming odds leaves little room to attribute their relatively low levels of educational attainment to uncongenial cultural values or educational norms. That more was not achieved means little, for the conditions have been appallingly difficult. (285)

In his discussion of Black education from 1950 to the mid-seventies, Meyer Weinberg (1977) makes a similar comment:

> Constituting a movement whose moral grandeur cast a light far beyond
> their own ranks, blacks raised anew many questions of the public good. In
> education, the idea of the public school was tested once more. . . . A cen-
> tury after emancipation, the schools for blacks were unemancipated
> still—often separate, unequal, dehumanized. The miracle was that the
> belief in learning among blacks had not been contained or suppressed.
> Each time hope was crushed, by the courts or legislature or the educa-
> tional establishment, it rose again. Occasionally, as in [*Brown* v. *Board of
> Education*] or the Civil Rights Act, public institutions supported this
> hope, encouraging expectation that, even when unfulfilled, nurtured
> new demands for equal and unsegregated education. Those who de-
> plored low academic achievement among black children seldom ac-
> knowledged that, given circumstances of overwhelming educational
> oppression, it was miraculous that any survived. (139)

What Ogbu fails to explore is the operative philosophy of schooling that has historically, over time—as we saw illustrated earlier in the
narratives—supported the development and sustenance of effort optimism among African Americans as a historically oppressed group: education for freedom, racial uplift, citizenship, and leadership. It is this
philosophy that is captured in the *Autobiography of Malcolm X,* in the
slave narratives, in the graduation scene in Maya Angelou's *I Know
Why the Caged Bird Sings,* in the African-American narrative tradition, and in the history of Black education. It is this stance toward education that has fueled the overrepresentation of African Americans
among America's best-known public intellectuals. It is this philosophy that over generations, has motivated African Americans to urge
their children to commit themselves to academic excellence, to attend college, even if, like my best friend's mother, who graduated
from Xavier University, it meant working as an elevator operator, or
for countless others, as Pullman porters, or in the post office.

One would have to concede that the social mobility theory does
appear to have greater explanatory power than the cultural difference
theory. The theory does explain some but not nearly all of the differential achievement patterns between immigrant and castelike minorities. Ogbu is correct in challenging the explanatory power of the
traditional representation of the cultural difference explanation for
the school performance of American's racial minorities. The articulation of the cultural difference theory, then and now, is too often repre-

sented as a no-fault situation, with the relationship of culture to power rendered invisible, underemphasized, or ignored.

Though not articulated as such, central to Ogbu's social mobility theory is the notion that America's racial minorities do not occupy the same sociopolitical position in the larger society. Ogbu errs, however, in dismissing culture as an important and predictive variable in the school performance of African Americans. Just because having a different culture doesn't appear to function as a barrier to the school performance for some racial minorities (such as Asian Americans) doesn't mean that it is not a barrier for others. If, as Ogbu argues, racial minorities occupy different sociopolitical positions in the larger society, it would stand to reason that their respective cultural formations do not carry the same social, ideological, or political salience. Stated simply, the cultures of Chinese Americans and Korean Americans do not have the same meaning, politically or ideologically, as the culture of African Americans. Black cultural formations—whether jazz, blues, or hip-hop—have always been viewed and taken on as symbols of rebellion, even by Asians and Asian Americans. Black cultural formations have been and continue to be inherently political, leading to the necessity of forging an explanatory model for the school performance of racial minorities, for African Americans, that includes a more sophisticated, nuanced, historically and politically grounded notion of culture—one that is necessarily linked to history and social and political location.

THE BLACK ENGLISH CASE AND THE SOCIAL MOBILITY AND CULTURAL DIFFERENCE THEORIES

The cultural difference theory formed the basis for the argumentation and intervention mandated by the court on behalf of the plaintiffs in the high-profile *Martin Luther King Jr.* v. *Ann Arbor School Board* case, the 1978 Black English case. I have chosen to focus on this case in the context of my discussion of the relative power of the cultural difference theory and the social mobility theory because the circumstances surrounding this case and the evidence contained in the testimony serve as a critique of Ogbu's too-easy dismissal of culture (beyond his definition of oppositional culture) as a variable in the school performance of African Americans. It also suggests that a more complicated analysis of how culture mediates inequality in an allegedly open, integrated society might be in order. At bottom, though it was not framed using these terms at the time of its occurrence, this case was about the gap in the achievement at the Martin Luther King Jr. Elementary School between the predominantly middle- and upper-class white students and the poor Black students who lived in Green Road Housing Development, a scattered public housing project. The poor Black parents whose complaints found expression in the legal suit were concerned about the inequality of educational outcomes. They had access to one of the best school systems in the country, but their children were not learning. It is worth noting that twenty years later the defendant class in the *Martin Luther King Jr.* v. *Ann Arbor School Board* case, the Ann Arbor School District, is one of the liberal, upper-middle-class districts that is now part of the Minority Achievement Network, a group of districts organized to address the achievement gap in their respective school systems. Over two decades earlier, in Ann Arbor, Michigan, Black parents had asked the system to focus on unequal outcomes, on the achievement gap.

The *Martin Luther King Jr.* v. *Ann Arbor School Board* case was brought on behalf of fifteen poor Black children who lived in the Green Road Housing Development in Ann Arbor, Michigan. The Martin Luther King Jr. School had labeled or attempted to label as learning disabled two-thirds of the Black children in attendance at the Martin Luther King Jr. School who lived in the Green Road Housing Development. According to the plaintiff's attorney, the reading levels of the children from the Green Road Housing Development were so low that they were in danger of becoming functionally illiterate. Although the upper age limit of the plaintiff children was eleven, not one of the plaintiff children was reading above the second grade level.

In the brief filed on behalf of the plaintiff children, the plaintiff attorney argued as follows: that the plaintiff children spoke Black English as their home language, that this language had not been acknowledged by the school, that it had been stigmatized, and as a result of this stigmatization a language barrier had been created between the children and the school staff. The attorney further argued that this stigmatization had impeded the progress of the students and their development of literacy and that there were actions that could properly be termed appropriate that the school should have taken to eliminate the language barrier.

In their briefs and in their argumentation, the plaintiff attorneys relied heavily on the testimony and expertise of linguists and sociolinguists, whose work was grounded in the cultural difference theory. The court ruled in favor of the plaintiffs and mandated as a remedy in-service training for the teachers, training in which they would learn about Black language and appropriate teaching and assessment strategies for students for whom Black English was their home language. The judge also relied on the expertise of the cultural difference theorists in his decision and in the remedy mandated.

What happened to the plaintiff children (captured in the testimony of the children and their teachers), specifically how the teachers reacted to their language, offers a compelling critique of the notion that African-American culture is not powerfully implicated in the school performance of African-American youth. The court documents provide clear evidence that the language the children spoke was stigmatized. The children did see their white schoolmates as able to "speak good," while they and their families were not able to "speak good." The children had been sent to speech therapy classes because they spoke Black language; the language they spoke had influenced their being assessed as learning disabled. Indeed, as the cultural difference theorists had suggested, Black language, although it did not need to be a barrier, was a barrier because of what it represented to teachers and the reactions it elicited from them. It was problematic because the teachers did not have the knowledge base or attitudes necessary to be able to distinguish between language difference and language disability.

While the facts of the case provide a powerful critique of Ogbu's dismissal of culture as a variable in the school performance of African Americans, they also point to the limitations of the traditional articulation of the cultural difference theory. It was not just that there existed a cultural mismatch between the children's home culture and the culture of the school; more to the point, cultural adaptation was functioning as a prerequisite for skill acquisition. I am not here suggesting that developing fluency in the dominant culture should not be an agenda for the school. But I do want to highlight the philosophy and practice that proceed on the assumption that a certain level of cultural adaptation necessarily precedes skill development and intellectual competency. This is very different from the philosophy and practice that were prevalent in many historically Black southern segregated schools, where developing academic competencies and fluency in mainstream culture were pursued as simultaneous rather than sequential processes.

Further, Pierre Bourdieu's (1970) notion of cultural capital provides a way to think about how culture mediated inequality in this allegedly open, integrated, progressive school community—not just for the poor Black children who were part of the lawsuit, but also for the middle-class Black children who attended the Martin Luther King Jr. School. These students were also underachieving in comparison with the white children, though not as dramatically. It provides a way for us to think about unequal achievement in those schools that are part of the Minority Achievement Network in a way that goes beyond the predictable focus on teacher expectations, tracking, and school achievement being incompatible with being Black.

According to Bourdieu (1970), cultural capital is socially inherited cultural competence that facilitates achievement in school. It is unequally distributed, and like economic capital it has an exchange value. In other words, culture, whether viewed as objective forms (books, works of art), practices (museum visits, concerts), or the institutional currency of academic credentials, is susceptible to treatment in terms of the laws governing macro- and microeconomic relationships. Cultural capital is competence passed on through primary socialization, "modes of use and relationship in language; relationship to and affinity for the dominant culture; styles of interaction and varying dispositions toward schooling itself."

It is important to recognize that for Bourdieu the mechanism for distributing educational opportunity resides in the academic culture, not in the characteristics of the social classes. Accordingly, schools transmit knowledge in cultural codes, which afford automatic advantages to those who already possess cultural and linguistic capital and disadvantages to those who possess little or no cultural capital. The existing educational system, given its interrelationship with the dominant culture and the close affinity between the dominant and the academic cultures, has already picked the winners. A cultural code is necessary to appropriate the message systems contained in cultural manifestations. According to Bourdieu,

> Successful academic apprenticeship depends on previous possession of the instruments of appropriation—*unless the school system explicitly and deliberately hands over in its pedagogic communication those instruments which are essential to the success of the communication and which, in a society divided into classes, are unequally distributed.* An educational system that puts into practice an implicit pedagogic action requiring initial familiarity with the dominant culture, and which proceeds by imperceptible familiarization, offers information and training which can only be received and acquired by subjects supported by the systems of predispositions which is the condition for the success of the transmission and inculcation of the culture. By doing away with giving explicitly to everyone what is implicitly demanded of everyone, the education system expects of everyone alike that they have what it does not give, which consist mainly of linguistic and cultural competence. (Bourdieu 1970, 3; emphasis added)

Now Bourdieu is arguing that instruction can be organized such that a child is automatically advantaged or disadvantaged, if he or she comes to school with a lot or a little cultural capital. Let me give the reader some examples of what this might mean in the concrete.

Scenario 1. Suppose there is a kindergarten or first grade teacher who decides to read this wonderful book to her children. The book has been assessed by all—children's literature specialists, teacher educators, and teachers—as an excellent piece of children's literature, one that should definitely be introduced to kindergarten and first grade children. The teacher reads the book to her children, and she does so appropriately. She asks questions and tries to elicit responses from the children. She calls their attention to the pictures, to the art, and so on. But despite all of her efforts, the children are not engaged. They are quiet, attentive, but not engaged. The content of the book, and the knowledge assumed, are so distant from the experiences of the children that the book fails to engage them. Never mind that the book is wonderful and ideal in every other regard. Now this needn't have been the case. The teacher could have done some prior work with the children before she read the book. She could have explicitly and systematically handed over to them the concepts and experiences that they needed in order for the reading of the text to be meaningful and engaging, connecting the text to the children's experiences. She also could have chosen one of the many multicultural texts that are great pieces of literature and developmentally appropriate to teach the language and concepts she was trying to teach with the book that failed to engage the children. But she could also have used the original book and employed a pedagogy similar to that used by another kindergarten and first grade teacher when she was teaching a unit on Ancient Greece, and more particularly as she began to teach about Greek architecture in the context of this unit.

Scenario 2. In order to prepare for teaching about Greek architecture, this young teacher, unbeknownst to her children, took pictures of every one of their homes. She then put all of these pictures on slides. When she actually began to teach about Greek architecture, she would point to the columns, the gables, and other features of the architecture that were present in their homes, as well as in Greek architecture. The vocabulary that emerged from this unit was meaningful, not only in the context of the unit on Greek architecture, but also in the context of descriptions of the children's homes, homes of their peers, and the architecture in their community.

This same teacher has arranged monthly visits to the Museum of Fine Arts for her kindergarten and first grade pupils. By February of the academic year, her students were more comfortable in the museum and knew more about what was in the museum than the average college student. Monthly visits to the museum had become an accepted ritual, "a practice." In both of these instances, the teacher was explicitly passing on to her students cultural capital. And she had also organized instruction such that a prior level of cultural capital was not necessary for her students to access, to fully benefit from, her instruction.

Scenario 3. A third grader is participating in a city-to-suburb busing program, one she has been involved in since kindergarten. The suburban school system is touted as being one of the best in the country. The girl's teacher tells her mother that she thinks her daughter might need to be assessed for special needs placement. The child is assessed, and contrary to the teacher's expectations, the assessment doesn't support a special needs placement. The child scores above grade level. But what is even more enlightening is the mother's conversation with the teacher who had recommended the special needs assessment. The teacher is concerned that the child doesn't know what a canoe is. The mother tells the teacher that her daughter does know what a boat is. The teacher further comments that the child didn't know what a polliwog was. The mother lets the teacher know that she doesn't either and asks the teacher what is it. The teacher responds by informing the mother that it is a tadpole. The mother tells the teacher that her daughter does know what a tadpole is. It is clear from this interaction that the teacher's judgment about the intellectual competence of the child is based of the child's possession of linguistic and cultural capital. Further, the fact that the student did not know the answers to the questions, after having been in the suburban system since kindergarten, suggests that her teachers had probably not explicitly handed over to her the cultural capital needed to fully benefit from the curriculum.

By way of contrast, the teacher in scenario 2 is introducing her students to a unit she has developed on the interaction between Asians and Africans along the Silk Road. In the context of this unit, her children are talking about transportation by water and boats, all kind of boats. On their word walls are words for all kinds of boats—tugboat, sailboat, canoe, and whale boat—as well as words for parts of the boats. This teacher is aware that some of her children may not have had the experiences that would have allowed them to acquire the word knowledge to identify and distinguish between different types of boats. She again explicitly hands over to her children cultural capital. She does not, like the suburban teacher in scenario 3, or some of the teachers of the plaintiff children, make judgments about her children's intellectual competence based on whether they had prior possession of cultural and linguistic capital.

To summarize, the cultures of racial minorities in this country don't all have the same ideological, political, or social salience. The *Martin Luther King Jr.* v. *Ann Arbor School Board* case provides ample evidence that the culture of African Americans, via language, is implicated in the school performance of African Americans. In this case, and in many other instances, Black language and communication style influence teachers' judgments about the intellectual capabilities of African-American children. This is not surprising when you consider the many studies that have documented that speakers of Black language are thought to be intellectually incompetent. It is not surprising when one reflects on a recent study in which, in telephone inquiries about advertised apartment vacancies, individuals were told that the apartments were unavailable if the language the inquirer spoke was identifiable as Black speech. These study results are illustrative of some realities suggested in the title of Lisa Delpit's most recent book, *The Skin That We Speak*.

But the examples cited provide only a partial look at how culture is implicated in the school performance of the children from the Green Road Housing Development, and indeed the school performance of all Black children who attend what appear to be open, integrated, progressive school systems, where individuals don't seem to be bent on denying equal opportunity to Black children. Indeed, a certain level of cultural adaptation does appear to influence the teacher's assessment of whether the children are ready to learn and can be taught. It also seems that the concept of cultural capital gives us a way to understand how in environments where students seem to be the beneficiaries of the same input, in terms of both content and pedagogy, instruction can be designed to afford automatic advantages to children who come to school with a lot of cultural capital.

BLACK IMMIGRANTS, IMMIGRANTS OF COLOR, AND AFRICAN AMERICANS

Now let us return to Ogbu's categorization of American racial minorities as immigrant and castelike minorities, which, based on the terms of their incorporation into the United States, is predictive of the much of the differential achievement patterns among racial minorities. Ogbu does not consider how immigrant status is affected by "being Black," by the social class and educational attainment of a significant portion of the immigrant group, by the power relationship between the country of origin and the United States, and by the sociohistorical and economic entry point of the immigrant group. Nor does Ogbu consider how immigrant status is affected by society's beliefs—no, ideology—about the intellectual capability of the immigrant group. Ogbu's explanatory model doesn't consider how "being Black" affects the school performance of Africans in America, whether one is a member of an immigrant or a castelike minority group. It does not consider how "being Black" affects how people in and out of school perceive one's intellectual work and ability.

Further, and related to the preceding point, the social mobility theory doesn't address the variations in achievement among immigrant minorities. Although it is generally acknowledged that Black immigrants do better in school than African Americans, Black immigrants don't perform nearly as well as Asian immigrants. To what extent is this differential a function of the widespread belief that Asians are smart? I would contend that while being a Black immigrant might advantage one in relationship to African Americans, the marker of skin color and what it represents in the white imagination inevitably cancels out some, but clearly not all, of the benefits that accrue from being an immigrant. The larger society's ideology of Black intellectual inferiority just has to moderate the effort optimism that comes with being an immigrant minority. It seems clear from Mary Waters's (1999) research on West Indian immigrants that "race as a master status in the United States soon overwhelms the identities of immigrants and their children as they are seen as Black Americans" (Waters 1999, 5). Most important in the context of this discussion, while the categories of immigrant and castelike minorities are important, they do not capture the complexities of what it means to be Black in this country or the role African Americans have assumed, historically and in the present, in the construction of what it means to be white in the United States.

THE SOCIAL CONSTRUCTION OF WHITENESS

Historians and social scientists have argued that race and ethnicity are not natural categories, but social constructions. Using Irish Americans as a paradigm for white racial formation, David Roediger (1991) and Noel Ignatiev (1995) contend that whiteness is a social construction with a cultural corollary. Roediger locates the construction of whiteness during the period between the American Revolution and the Civil War. With the rise of republicanism, independence emerged as a white male value; at the same time, the spread of wage labor brought with it a fear of dependence. According to Roediger, the construction of whiteness provided a way for the white working class to deal with these competing claims. And "in a society in which Black and servility were so intertwined, assertions of white freedom could not be raceless" (Roediger 1991, 49). White male workers defined themselves in counterpoint to Blacks—to be white was to be not-Black. According to Roediger, white workers dealt with their fear of dependency on wage labor by distancing themselves and their labor from that of Blacks, substituting new terms for those that reflected servile relations—"boss" for master, "help" for servant, and "laborer" for hireling.

Whiteness has a cultural as well as an ideological component. In discussing minstrelsy, Roediger draws on the work of Herbert Gutman (1976), who documented how difficult it was for white workers to adapt to the discipline of industrial capitalism, and on George Rawick's (1972) and Nathan Huggins's (1971) interpretations of minstrelsy. Roediger describes minstrelsy as "the tendency of racist entertainers to project white male anxieties onto black face characters," providing a way for white workers to reconcile longings for their preindustrial past with their newly required discipline. By projecting onto Blacks their present and past longings, white workers via minstrelsy created pornography of Black life. According to Roediger (1991, 14), "disciplined and made anxious by fear of dependency," the white working class constructed "an image of the Black population as 'other'—as embodying the pre-industrial, erotic, careless lifestyle the white worker hated and longed for. This logic had particular attractiveness for Irish American immigrant workers, even as the 'whiteness' of these very workers was under dispute."

Thus Ignatiev, Roediger, and others contend that "whiteness" is not a natural category, but an ideological construction with a cultural corollary. "Whiteness" was created in opposition to how "Blackness" was imagined. To be "white" was to be "not-slave," "not-Black."

Decades ago, Ralph Ellison (1972) wondered about white youth who were enthralled with the music of Stevie Wonder yet would shout racial slurs at African Americans if they came onto their white-only beaches. Roediger (1993) wondered about contemporary youth who wear "Public Enemy" caps and at the same time sport belts emblazoned with the Confederate flag. Historically located in the latter half of the nineteenth century, this complex mixture of longing and hate, which is central to the construction of "whiteness," extends to the present via contemporary minstrelsy and race bending. The arrival of hip-hop music on the popular culture scene has "created an entire subclass of wannabes . . . as millions of white fans of Black rappers have adopted modes of dress, speech, and a style that they consider Black." We have also witnessed the emergence of groups like the Beastie Boys, House of Pain, and more recently Eminem and Bubba Sparks, white rappers "whose strut and postures are 'blacker' than most of their fans, even more so than most Blacks" (Ledbetter 1992, 112). These groups reflect the sentiment expressed by Janis Joplin years ago when she uttered that she just wanted to be Black for a while. Cornel West has termed this phenomenon "the Afro-Americanization of youth culture." Like the minstrels in times past, these youth, even in their blackface, continue to participate in white privilege. Youth can don blackface, but our institutions usually don't, even public schools in urban America with a significant Black student body. In spite of the Afro-Americanization of popular culture and current thinking that posits that American culture and its canonical literature is critically informed by the African-American presence (Morrison 1989a, b), most of our educational institutions continue to institutionalize "whiteness" as the culture of power. Even as white people might be attracted to Black culture—whether jazz, hip-hop, the plays of August Wilson or Suzan-Lori Parks, the literature of Toni Morrison, or Langston Hughes—these same people are often repulsed when the aesthetic that is represented in these artistic expressions is presented in the Black body of Black children, and especially Black youth. One can easily imagine that the con artist characters audiences fell in love with in Suzan-Lori Parks's Pulitzer Prize–winning *Topdog/ Underdog* wouldn't get such a warm response if they weren't fictional, if their loud speech was on the street instead of in a theater.

How should this discussion of "whiteness" and our reflection on the *Martin Luther King Jr. v. Ann Arbor School Board* case inform the recasting of the cultural difference explanation of school failure? How should it inform the inclusion of a robust and politically grounded notion of culture in the development of an explanatory model for African-American achievement? How can it be used to further respond to Ogbu's failure to include culture as a predictor of African-

American school performance? If "whiteness" is constructed politically and culturally in opposition to "Blackness," African-American culture will have a different cultural meaning in school and in society from the culture of other racial minorities. In thinking about how culture is implicated in school performance, the cultures of racial minorities might be viewed as on a continuum, with Black culture at one end and white culture at the other. To the extent that the culture of a racial minority approximates "Blackness as symbol" and those cultural features associated with "Blackness" in the white imagination, to that extent will culture be problematic for that minority. Stated another way, "whiteness" was not constructed in opposition to "Asianness" or "Puerto Rican-ness," but in opposition to how "Blackness" was imagined. Thus it is not surprising that in the white imagination the qualities associated with being Asian American are the polar opposite to those associated with being African American. In the white imagination, to be Asian American is to be studious, reserved, hardworking, law abiding, polite, respectful of one's elders, and a member of a strong family. In the white imagination, to be African American is to be lazy, criminal, from broken families, rebellious, emotional, and disrespectful of authority.

To revise Bourdieu's notion of cultural capital, and incorporating an understanding of the dialectics of race and class culture in American society, African-American children are afforded advantages if they possess not only cultural capital as defined by Bourdieu (dispositions, tastes, values, "habitas," institutionalized as the culture of power), but also a subset of those cultural features that represent "whiteness" in the American imagination, which has been defined in counterpoint to how "Blackness" is imagined. I hypothesize that these include the ability to be reserved, to subordinate emotions and affections to reason, to constrain physical activity, and to present a disciplined exterior. Cultural capital in the context of this country, particularly when applied to African Americans, necessarily includes these characteristics. Conversely, African Americans are disadvantaged if in their expressive culture they project those African-American cultural formations that are viewed as oppositional to what it means to be white.

African Americans are implicated in the political and cultural definition of what it means to be white like no other racial minority. This is captured in the research of sociologist Mary Waters (1999) on West Indian immigrants. It is usually understood by immigrants that if they are going to move up in the society they will have to get rid of the markers of their ethnicity. Afro-Caribbean immigrants, however, have a different understanding. They understand that in order to move up in the society they will need to retain or accentuate those characteristics that clearly mark them as immigrants. They understand that their chances of moving up in the society are enhanced if they can distance themselves from African Americans, "the fundamental other." Some West Indians thus go to some effort to retain their accent or to display flags or ornaments that clearly mark them as not African American. Waters also documents that this understanding has a material basis, as employers demonstrate a preference for Black immigrants over African Americans. And if what it means to be white is constructed in opposition to how blackness is imagined (meaning African Americans), then African Americans are implicated in the consciousness of white Americans like no other minority. Gail Dines (personal communication, May 1997) argues that all other racial minorities have the possibility of negotiating themselves out of blackness, symbolically defined as the fundamental other, except African Americans because of they/we are necessarily embedded in very notion of what it means to be white.

Thus I would argue that Ogbu doesn't seem to demonstrate an understanding of the special status of African Americans in the cultural and political reality of this country, nor does he have an understanding of the role of African Americans in the construction of what it means to be white. He also doesn't seem to understand that while Black immigrants benefit from their immigrant status, they are always at risk of losing their status as Black immigrants. Black immigrants know this. Because of the marker of skin color, they are always in danger of being seen as African Americans. And they resist this at every turn. At the same time, they are a good stand-in for African Americans, particularly for white Americans who feel they owe African Americans something, but for whom Black immigrants are more acceptable or tolerable. This phenomenon may account for the overrepresentation of Black immigrants among Black affirmative action admittees at Ivy League and elite colleges and universities.

EFFORT OPTIMISM AND
AFRICAN-AMERICAN EPISTEMOLOGY

Ogbu's theoretical perspective relies significantly on the notion that because education has not resulted in commensurate job-market rewards for castelike minorities African Americans have developed a lack of effort optimism. It seems reasonable that maintaining effort optimism would be critical for a historically oppressed people. Evidence suggests that maintaining effort optimism is both a dilemma and an adaptive behavior, even for successful African-American professionals in mainstream society (Benjamin 1991; Edwards and Polite 1992). If this is a dilemma for African-American adults, it is a pretty good guess that maintaining effort optimism would be a psychological issue of significant import for African-American schoolchildren, particularly if they experience discrimination in both school and society without the benefit of environments or institutions offering rituals, practices, and orientations that are intentionally organized to develop and sustain effort optimism.

Further, it seems eminently reasonable for us to ask what it is that has historically sustained African Americans' desire to get an education and to achieve. I believe that an answer to this question can be found by turning, as we did in part 1, to the intellectual, historical, and narrative traditions of African Americans and asking about their beliefs about education. What constructions were powerful enough to motivate and sustain the development of a class of Black intellectuals, to sustain in African Americans the desire for school achievement? The philosophy of education, "freedom for literacy and literacy for freedom," that has developed and sustained optimism among many African Americans across generations has also created a class of public intellectuals from slavery to the present. Whether literary or legal scholars, philosophers, educators, or historians, African Americans feel the need to speak out on the dominant issues affecting the democracy. In our age, we know them as bell hooks, Cornel West, Derrick Bell, Toni Morrison, Henry Louis Gates, Jim Anderson, Asa Hilliard, Patricia Williams, and Michael Dyson, to name a few. I hypothesize that the African-American philosophy of schooling has motivated the emergence of a disproportionately high number of contemporary public intellectuals.

If our society is still characterized by particularly virulent racism against African Americans, by an ideology of Black intellectual and cultural inferiority, and by structured inequality (Essed 1991; Benjamin 1991; Scott 1991; Ward 1991; Edwards and Polite 1992), could it be that the predominant philosophy of education of the pre–Civil Rights era remains the only philosophy of education with sufficient power to develop and sustain within a majority of African Americans the desire to achieve in school? In our post–Civil Rights era, to what extent and among what generations of African Americans has the African-American philosophy of education for freedom, leadership, citizenship, and racial uplift been retained? The answer is unclear. Indeed, the African-American intellectual tradition suggests that schooling for work is probably not transcendent enough, powerful enough, sufficient to sustain, in African Americans as a historically oppressed group, the desire to achieve in school in our present society, where the ideology of Black intellectual inferiority still reigns.

It is true that the lack of a predictable correspondence between effort and reward would almost certainly affect one's motivation. But what I am terming the dilemma of achievement for African Americans is located in experiences that are not tied singularly to intergenerational labor market experiences. The dilemma of achievement is located in the society's ideology about African Americans' intellectual and cultural inferiority. It is located in African-American children's day-to-day experience of racism in the larger society, in stores, in schools, in restaurants, and in other public places (Essed 1991). Deborah Mathis's (2002) description of what it means for African Americans to still not to be at home in America expresses why the dilemma of achievement can't be restricted to labor market experiences. According to Mathis,

> Except during outbreaks of vicious bigotry, it is difficult to persuade white America that the alienation of Black America is actual and ongoing, afflicting each generation through policy, custom, quack science, and if nothing else, the Look. We learn to recognize the Look very early in life. It radiates from white strangers' faces. It's not the same look of benign curiosity that is cast upon the typical newcomer, but a distinct look of unease, confusion, dislike, disapproval, alarm, dread, even hatred. And it conveys myriad questions—What are you doing here? What do you want? What are you up to?—while making one unmistakable appeal: go

away. . . . If you are hit by it early in life or often enough, the Look can
kill. Not your body, but your spirit. Kill your faith that you will ever belong. Kill your hopes that what you have to offer the world will ever be
noticed, appreciated, nurtured, or rewarded. Kill your desire to participate, to go along, to get along. Snuff out your will to even try. (Mathis
2002, 15, 16)

Even if education leads to a good job, even if African-American
parents communicate clearly to their children that education pays off,
these experiences can be neutralized if children experience school
and the larger society as unfair and discriminatory. In other words, a
child's belief in the power and importance of schooling and intellectual work can be interrupted by teachers and others who explicitly
or subtly convey a disbelief in the child's ability for high academic
achievement, and the child having a rightful place in the larger society—unless a counternarrative about the child's identity as an intellectual being is intentionally passed on to him or her.

The dilemma of achievement for African Americans is tied to (a)
their identity as members of a castelike minority group; (b) the larger
society's ideology of Black intellectual inferiority and its reproduction in the mass media and in everyday interactions; (c) their identity
as members of a group whose culture is seen, by all segments of the society, even other people of color, as simultaneously inferior and attractive; and (d) their identity as American citizens. The dilemmas
contained in these realities, which were presented in this essay's introduction, make the task of achievement for African Americans distinctive.

Just as the African-American philosophy of schooling is richly expressed in the African-American narrative tradition, also embedded
in these narratives are stories about how African Americans over the
years have experienced the dilemma of achievement. The dilemma is
expressed in the *Autobiography of Malcolm X,* when Malcolm X is told
by Mr. Ostrowski to be realistic and not aspire to be a lawyer. It is present in the narrative of Gwendolyn Parker when she was told by her
teacher that she could not possibly have written the poem she submitted for her class assignment. It is present in the interview with Haki
Madhubuti when he recalls how the sergeant snatched from his hand
the book that he was reading about Paul Robeson, tore the pages out,
and gave pages to the other recruits, telling them to use them for toilet

paper. Indeed, contained in the oral and written narrative tradition of the African American is an abundance of stories about how over the years African Americans have experienced the dilemma of achievement. Yes, the dilemma of achievement can be located in the labor market experiences of African Americans, but this is but one location for a global experience. And herein we can level the same critique at Ogbu that he levels against the cultural difference theorists: In discussing the experiences that are implicated in the lack of effort optimism among African Americans, instead of focusing broadly on the lived experiences of African Americans, Ogbu overemphasizes their discrete and intergenerational labor market experiences.

DUAL SOCIOPOLITICAL IDENTITIES

The African-American intellectual tradition is replete with testimonies of individuals who have grappled with the dilemma of reconciling one's dual sociopolitical identities—American and African American; member and outsider; citizen, but without the rights and privileges of full citizenship (Johnson 1912; Wright 1968; McClain 1986; Benjamin 1991; Edwards and Polite 1992; Early 1993). In *The Souls of Black Folk,* W. E. B. Du Bois (1989) speaks about "two souls, two thoughts, two unreconciled strivings, two warring ideals in one dark body, whose dogged strength alone keeps it from being torn asunder" (5). Chester Pierce (1989), a psychiatrist at the Harvard Medical School, talks about the balancing act required to function as member and as outsider, as the subject and as the object of racism. He queries,

> How and when do we accommodate to racism versus how and when do we resist racism? Our constant problem is when and how do we seek assimilation in the total society, versus when and how do we insist on separation from the total society? Our ongoing existential doubt is whether we are warmly welcomed or merely tolerated by the general community. The psychological resolution of these conflicts on either a group or individual basis claims an extraordinary amount of our time and effort. The nature of the resolution is framed always by racism's inhibitors that define the limits of hope, desire, probability and possibility. (296)

In Lois Benjamin's study (1991) of the racism experienced by one hundred Black professionals, she finds that 93 percent "believe that double consciousness leads to identity confusion and inherent contradictions in the collective psyche of peoples of African descent" (5). The narratives of African-American professionals who have experienced this double consciousness suggest a powerful continuity with the perspective of Du Bois (1989), so much so that one of her interviewees commented, "The thing that is so discouraging is that when I read Du Bois' writings published in 1898, I would still think it was 1989 if you didn't tell me the year it was written, and that's when you feel it's sad" (4). Consider the following reflections on double consciousness taken from Benjamin's study:

Informant No. 1
It presents a divided loyalty of wanting to belong, to love one's country, and wanting to be proud of it, but always being somewhat a stranger about one's own experience here. It forces Blacks to choose between [being] Black or American and being forced to choose is destroying part of one's self.

Informant No. 2
When you think of yourself as an American, America doesn't think of you as an American. That's the problem. Sometimes you are forced to go back to your blackness, because America won't let you be an American, even though that's the way I grew up thinking. I am going to be smart. I am going to school and make it in society. You get a lot of knocks on your head by Whites in society, reminding you after all you are Black. Everything that's for me isn't for you as a Black. That's the real problem—a Catch-22.

Informant No. 3
I'll never forget that experience when I was in Brazil at an international festival for the arts, where they brought Black folks from seventeen different countries. And we were in the hotel and different people were talking about their countries. As things developed, a Nigerian said, "I love my country." A Cuban said, "I love my country." A Panamanian said, "I love my country." I couldn't say that, and I have been here all my life. I've accomplished and I've suffered, but I would be hesitant to say I love this country.

Informant No. 4
Not since my early impressionable elementary school stage have I really

felt pride and patriotism. The rude awakening of the need to constantly struggle for constitutionally guaranteed rights leaves a very bitter taste and a permanent sense of alienation and insecurity. Blacks constantly face issues of racism at home. This reality is so draining.

It is currently fashionable for intellectuals of different racial and cultural backgrounds to view the dilemma of being American and African American as a nonadaptive cultural construction. Although some African Americans acknowledge the persistence of this dilemma, others see it as a "muddle of ideas that purport to explicate an alienation between national and racial identity, casting them as warring ideas" (Crouch 1993, 84). However, Laraine Morin grounds this dilemma in her "lived experience":

> In one of my graduate school courses there were twenty-four of us, all of us experienced teachers, most of us in our thirties. I was the only Black person in the course, in fact, the only one in the program. One day we did an exercise in which everyone had to point out on a map where their families had come from. I was the only one out of that group whose grandparents, all four of them, had been born in the U.S. I realized then that if anyone had roots in this country, it was me. I was "All American," a claim that nobody else in the room could make. At the same time, we all knew who was the most marginalized, who would be viewed in most circumstances with the most suspicion, whose capability and competency would be most questioned. (Morin et al. 1993, 42)

THE PSYCHOLOGY OF BICULTURALITY IN POST–CIVIL RIGHTS SOCIETY

The need and desire to be bicultural has traditionally functioned as a given among African Americans and has been institutionalized in their schools and community institutions. According to Lisa Delpit (1993), African-American professionals who attended historically Black schools remember teachers who were unambivalent about their need to become bicultural, specifically to acquire fluency in the dominant discourse.

> Their teachers successfully taught . . . the "superficial features" of middle-class Discourse—grammar, style, mechanics. . . . And the students successfully learned them. These teachers also successfully taught

the more subtle aspects of dominant Discourse . . . that students be able to speak and write eloquently, maintain neatness, think carefully, exude character, and conduct themselves with decorum. They even found ways to mediate class difference by attending . . . to the hygiene of students who needed such attention—washing faces, cutting fingernails and handing out deodorant. . . . . All of these teachers were able to teach in classrooms the rules for dominant Discourses, allowing students to succeed in mainstream America who were not only born outside of the realms of power and status, but who had no access to status institutions. These teachers were not themselves a part of the power elite, not members of dominant Discourses. Yet they were able to provide the keys for their students' entry into the larger world, never knowing if the doors would ever swing open to allow them in. (288–89)

Such clarity about the capacity and the need for biculturality might not necessarily function as a given in the culture and "lived experiences" of "desegregated" schools. But I would argue that clearly it should.

If we accept the historical work of Roediger (1991), that "whiteness" as cultural identity has been constructed precisely in opposition to Blackness as it is imagined, and if we also accept Wade Boykin and Forrest Toms's (1985) notion that those features associated with Blackness are devalued in mainstream society, it is important to explore the psychology of biculturality and its relationship to school achievement. What happens when the need for and possibility of biculturality is neither assumed nor institutionalized? What happens when African-American children's schooling experiences reinforce the oppositional character of African-American and mainstream culture? What role can the community play in affirming the possibility and nonoppositional character of biculturality?

In my observations of adult-child interactions I have seen how language can be the locus for biculturality. Among African-American mothers, I have observed attempts, sometimes with children as young as three, to standardize their syntax, if not their phonology. School can sometimes reinforce this pressure. During my regular visits home at Christmas, I found my five-year-old nephew, whose parents are fluent in African-American language and the standard code, after only four months in kindergarten, busily correcting the speech of family members when their phonological pronunciations differed from that of standard American English. He entered school with fluency in the syntax of standard American English and with the phonology and syntax of standard African-American language. After just four months in school, he had acquired a fair amount of fluency in standard phonology and now consistently corrected his mother. Demonstrating his newly acquired fluency became almost a game. If his mother said, "Close the doe," he would say, "*No, door.*" She would respond, "Ok, Javier, close the door." At five he had acquired fluency in standard American English and was experimenting with an understanding of its appropriate context.

Clearly, in his school in Birmingham, Alabama, the possibility of biculturality and bilingualism was a given. Although Javier's teachers were helping him to develop fluency in the standard code, they had done so in a way that did not imply a rejection of his home culture. But it has always been acknowledged in the African-American community that the use of mainstream or African-American language is contextual: one can be called "uppity" for using formal codes in nonformal settings, or castigated when nonformal codes intrude into formal settings (Murray 1978).

FROM ANALYSIS TO THEORY BUILDING

At this point, it is perhaps appropriate to ask what insights and orientations we can take from our conversation about the relative power of the cultural difference and the social mobility explanations for the school performance of racial minorities. What insights can be used to inform the development of a theory of African-American achievement?

Clearly one's social location—more specifically, being a member of a racial caste group—should be considered in the development of a theory of African-American achievement. But it is not simply the lack of a predictable relationship between school achievement and the rewards in the labor market that creates the dilemma of achievement. The ideology of African-American intellectual and cultural inferiority, as well as the many experiences in and out of school where there is an ambivalent response to effort, academic achievement, and responsible citizenship, are also implicated in the dilemma of achievement.

All people, including historically oppressed people and African Americans, are not simply the products of their environment and social location, but are also subjects. African Americans responded to the historically grounded dilemmas of achievement by developing and passing on the philosophy of schooling: freedom for literacy and literacy for freedom, racial uplift, citizenship, and leadership. This philosophy was transcendent and powerful enough to develop and sustain the desire to achieve in school, over generations, in a people for whom effort was not necessarily tied to comparable rewards, and for whom education and intellectual work was considered the antithesis of their identity as African Americans.

Culture has to figure centrally in the development of an explanatory model for the school performance of African Americans. The cultural formations of different racial minorities have different cultural and political salience in the larger society. Just as there is an ideology of Black intellectual inferiority, there is also an ideology of Black cultural inferiority. Furthermore, Black cultural formations are implicated in the very definition and construction of what it means to be "white." For as Roediger and Ignatiev would argue, whiteness is this complex mixture of longing and hate for Black cultural formations.

Thus it is quite clear that the presence of Black cultural formations in the context of school causes teachers to make judgments about a child's intellectual competence. Further, as suggested by the *Martin Luther King Jr.* v. *Ann Arbor School Board* case and the work of Pierre Bourdieu, in an allegedly open integrated society (in our post–Civil Rights society), cultural adaptation functions as a prerequisite to skill acquisition. Additionally, school is organized so as to afford automatic advantages to those who come to school with a lot of cultural capital and disadvantages to those with little cultural capital. In this context we would expand Bourdieu's definition of cultural capital to include not just dispositions, practices, language use, and experiences but also those qualities associated with what it means to be white in the American imagination—subordination of emotions to reason, the ability to present a disciplined exterior, and to constrain body movements.

Thus a theory of achievement for African Americans should be critically informed by African Americans' identity as a racial caste group, as a cultural group in opposition to which whiteness has been defined, and as putative members of mainstream society. Any theory of African-American achievement should help us understand and explain and predict success as well as failure, and should be such that it can point us in the direction of empirical studies that can confirm or suggest a revision of the proposed theoretical framework.

PART THREE

ACHIEVING IN POST–CIVIL RIGHTS AMERICA: THE OUTLINE OF A THEORY

In the introduction to this essay, I argued that, in thinking about African-American achievement, it was important for this conversation to be informed by an understanding of what we are asking African-American children to do, not just once, but over time, again and again, when we ask them to commit themselves to achieve in school. It is important that we understand the nature of the task of achievement for African Americans. I have further argued that the task of achievement is fundamentally shaped by the very identity of African Americans as African Americans. It is not different in minor ways or at the edges, but substantively a different task. I am not arguing that this task is fixed over time, for even as it is fundamentally shaped by the identity of African Americas as African Americas, it is also always changing as the sociopolitical context in which African Americans live, work, and go to school changes.

Thus we will begin this section by reflecting on and contrasting the task of achievement in the pre– and post–Civil Rights eras. Thereafter, drawing on an understanding of the task of achievement in the both of these eras as well as research studies, I will discuss what schools, communities, and teachers can do to promote academic achievement among African-American youth in the post–Civil Rights era. I will end by proposing an outline of a theory of achievement for African Americans that draws on the African-American philosophy of schooling as presented in part 1 and the understandings that emerged in part 2 from the critical analysis of the cultural difference and social mobility theories.

THINKING ABOUT ACHIEVEMENT
IN THE PRE—CIVIL RIGHTS ERA

In the pre–Civil Rights era, unequal educational opportunity was an uncontested reality. The ideology of white supremacy and black intellectual inferiority, in communities in the South and in some communities in other parts of the country, was quite explicit. Black people in the Jim Crow South knew that most white people saw them as intellectually inferior and less than human. Indeed, a whole complex of social relations, the exercise of power, and distribution of economic resources, goods, and services were organized in support of this ideological position. What white people and those in power thought about African Americans found expression in visible practices, in terms of whether and to what kind of schools African Americans had access, where African Americans could sit on buses, whether they could try on shoes in department stores, the kind of justice that was meted out by law enforcement officers and the criminal justice system, the lack of paved roads in the Black community, and so on.

In response to these realities, most if not all of the historically Black segregated schools that African-American children attended were intentionally organized in opposition to the ideology of Black intellectual inferiority. In other words, in addition to being sites of learning, they also instituted practices and expected behaviors and outcomes that not only promoted education—an act of insurgency in its own right—but also were also designed to counter the ideology of African Americans' intellectual inferiority and ideologies that saw African Americans as not quite equal and as less than human. Everything about these institutions was supposed to affirm Black humanity, Black intelligence, and Black achievement. I concur with James Scott, who argues that the act of constructing an institution whose organization and operation counter the larger society's ideology about an oppressed people is an act of resistance.

The idea of developing institutions and organizations that would intentionally counter the larger society's ideology about African Americans as intellectually inferior and less than human was embraced not only by the schools but also by other organizations and institutions in the community—churches, social clubs, and self-help organizations. It wasn't as if these institutions did not have their own specific goals—religious, social, or economic—it's just that whatever the explicit organizational goals, they were accomplished within the context of the larger and more important goal of affirming Black humanity, Black intelligence, Black achievement. The messages that a school chose to communicate were reinforced not simply by individuals outside the school, but by the other institutional formations in the community. Thus Joycelyn Elders could assert in her narrative that even though her mother and grandmother were unrelenting about the importance of getting an education, insisting that she had to get an education so that she could "be somebody," this message was communicated just as forcefully by her teachers at school and her minister in his sermons. In other words, there was triangulation of influences.

The teachers and principals of the segregated Black schools, often leaders in the African-American community writ large, who themselves lived the sociopolitical position of African Americans as a racial caste group, organized institutions that intentionally countered this positional identity. The teachers and principals promoted, in the context of the Jim Crow schools, practices—curricular, behavioral, ritualistic, and so on—designed to counter the status of African Americans as a racial caste group. It is important here to remember that organizations and institutions are not givens but social constructions. To a certain extent, they can be whatever a people decide they should be. And as Holland so eloquently reminds us,

> People have the propensity to be drawn to, recruited for, and formed in these worlds, and to become active and passionate about an imaginary universe (an intentional community). This is what makes oppression possible, it is also what makes it possible for a people to be liberated, to some extent, from the constraints of their environment. (Holland et al. 1998)

In *Cultural Identities and Social Worlds,* when discussing positional identities, Holland describes the experience of a Japanese-American anthropologist who had grown up in the United States and was doing fieldwork in Japan. One afternoon, the anthropologist went shopping at a time when most Japanese housewives would also be shopping. As she was shopping, strolling her baby, selecting vegetables, she caught a glimpse of herself in the "shiny metal surface of the butcher's display case." The anthropologist became disoriented. The image of herself in the butcher's display case so approximated the image of a "typical young Japanese housewife, clad in slip-on sandals, and the loose, cotton shift called 'homewear,' a woman walking with a characteristically Japanese bend to the knees and a sliding of the feet" (Holland et al. 1998, 139). The image in the butcher's display case was so different from the image the Japanese American had of herself that she became disoriented, as she could hardly believe that this was an image of herself. When seeing the reflection of herself, she realized that while immersing herself in her fieldwork, she had acquired the positional/gendered identity of a young Japanese housewife. Moreover, this had happened outside of her consciousness, without her realizing that it was happening.

In historically Black segregated schools that were intentionally organized to counter the positional identities of African-American students, teachers routinely promoted behaviors and practices that countered the identities of their students and students' parents as members of an oppressed people. Let me give several examples of how this was done. An outsider to the southern Jim Crow experience might be tempted to trivialize or misread attempts by Black teachers to promote behaviors designed to counter the students' positional identities. This is always tricky business, because there is a thin line between giving students the wherewithal to interact with fluency in the larger society and mimicry of those in power. Many African Americans who have grown up in the South can recall being told by their teachers on many occasions, "hold your head up high, throw your shoulders back, walk like you are somebody." This exhortation was not simply the admonition of a strict old schoolmarm. Having been reared in the Jim Crow South, I have always known intuitively that this exhortation was about asking us to carry ourselves as if we were free, asking us to refuse to allow our social location, our positional identity, to find expression in our bodies. When I spoke about this exhortation and my interpretation of it in a talk I gave several years ago in Evanston, Illinois, an African-American female teacher from the South, well into her eighties, remembered the many times she had said these same words to African-American students when teaching in the South, and to her African-American students after she had come north. Her interpretation of these remarks was that she was telling her students, without telling them in an explicit manner, not to carry their bodies like they would have if they had been working in the field or picking cotton. A colleague of mine tells a story about his son, who was raised in the Northeast, and who, having enrolled in a historically Black college, returned home for a visit after only a couple of months on the campus. My colleague said, "When he came home, he just walked differently, carried himself differently, with a surer step and more confidence." He attributed this change in his son's demeanor to the deliberate socialization that had occurred at the historically Black college. But whether this is true or not, we do know that even in the post–Civil Rights context, some historically Black colleges still feel the need to engage in practices designed to counter the positional identities of Black students. This is one of the reasons why so many middle- and upper-class African-American families in the post-Civil Rights era choose Black colleges for their children. And then there was the common practice at southern Black schools to include the singing of both the national anthem and the Negro national anthem at formal events, symbolically affirming that the students were simultaneously both fully members of the American democracy and outsiders, fighting for membership in American society.

One could describe the many behaviors and practices that were part of the very existence of the historically Black school. However, if one reduces these schools to behaviors and practices, one would miss the point. What the Black community did was to organize intentional educational communities, collectively constituted, "as-if" communities, imaginary communities that were capable of modeling possibilities. One can call historically Black schools "figured universes," or more precisely counterhegemonic figured communities.

These schools were counterhegemonic communities inasmuch as they were organized in opposition to the dominant ideology of white supremacy and Black intellectual inferiority. They were designed to forge the *collective* identity of African Americans as a literate and achieving people. Central to the formation of a counterhegemonic community is the continual articulation and passing on of a counternarrative. Several months ago, I was speaking to a young woman at my place of employment about why it has been so important for African-American youth to have a counternarrative about themselves and their possibilities, historically and most definitely now, at a time when the media is so centrally implicated in the formation of identities.

Her eyes glazed over and I wasn't quite sure if she understood what I was trying to say. But then the Grammy awards show was broadcast on network television. And the day afterward we were talking about Alicia Keyes, who had won many awards, and the person who, though nominated, we thought should have won one or several awards, India Arie. This young white woman, athletic, fit, short, attractive—but definitely not the larger society's image of an attractive white woman—began to sing the words from one of India Arie's songs: "I'm not your average girl from the video, my worth is not determined by the price of my clothes. My mama says a lady ain't what she wears but what she knows. . . ." She proceeded to tell me that just hearing the song made her feel better about herself. I immediately chimed in, "That's a counternarrative"—if it is passed on consistently and intentionally in a group setting.

The counternarrative that was passed on in the historically Black school and is contained in the African-American narrative tradition includes stories about struggles for literacy, stories about the purpose of literacy, stories about what people were willing to do to become literate, and stories about how people became literate so that they could "be somebody," lead their people, and register to vote. If it is true that freedom for literacy and literacy for freedom is the central theme that is contained in the African-American narrative tradition, as Henry Louis Gates and Robert Stepto have maintained and as I have attempted to illustrate in part 1, then what is equally important is that within these narratives, narrative is often directly implicated in the narrator's ability to commit himself or herself to education and achievement. Certainly, the stories that Gwendolyn Parker heard about her family and its achievements—the story about her great-grandfather getting the highest score on the state medical boards, her grandmother's stories to anybody who would listen about Gwendolyn being as smart, if not smarter, than her father—shaped her identity as an achiever. Indeed, according to Gwendolyn, these were not just her stories, but the stories of the entire community. Richard Wright's narrative changed Haki Madhubuti, and the story that Edith Folb told at the chapel at Philander-Smith College about her struggles and achievements as a doctor was pivotal in Joycelyn Elders's decision to become a doctor. Narratives or stories always figure centrally in the construction of identities. And the stories about achievement that

were passed on, informally and formally, whether in weekly assemblies, at church, or graduation ceremonies, were also involved in the
creation of the collective identity of African Americans as a literate,
achieving people. Not only were these stories reflective of who African Americans were, but they also ushered in and reconfirmed that
identity. The definition of identity that Holland and others provide
allows us to see why narrative is so central to the construction of identities. According to Holland,

> People tell others who they are, but even more important, they tell them-
> selves and then try to act as though they are who they say they are. These
> self-understandings, especially those with strong emotional resonance
> for the teller, are what we refer to as identities. . . .
>
> Identities are the key means by which people care about and care for
> what is going on around them.
>
> Identities are hard-won standpoints that, however dependent upon
> social support and however vulnerable to change, make at least a modi-
> cum of self-direction possible (Holland et al. 1998, 3, 4).

The historically Black school was conceived of as a *figured counter-*
hegemonic community. Again we turn to Holland for a definition of a
"figured world":

> By "figured world" we mean a socially and culturally constructed realm
> of interpretation in which particular characters and actors are recog-
> nized, significance is assigned to certain acts, and particular outcomes are
> valued over others. These collective "as-if" worlds are sociohistoric,
> contrived interpretations or imaginations that mediate behavior and so,
> from the perspective of heuristic development, inform participants' out-
> looks. (Holland et al. 1998, 52)

Historically Black schools were counterhegemonic in as much
as they institutionalized, ritualized, and symbolized the African-
American philosophy of schooling, forged in slavery and passed on
throughout history: "education for freedom, racial uplift, citizenship,
and leadership." When we say that this philosophy was institutionalized, we mean that it was the central meaning system that informed
institutional life in these schools and to which its participants would
to a greater or lesser extent be socialized. This philosophy was explicitly articulated, regularly ritualized, and passed on in formal public events (assemblies, graduations, May Day celebrations, etc.) and in

collectively constituted activities (clubs, organizations, etc.) that were markers of life in the school. In these counterhegemonic, figured communities, cultural artifacts were used to pass on, create, and reinforce beliefs and identities embedded in the African-American philosophy of schooling. Stories and narratives concretized the enactment of this philosophy over time, as well as in the present. These stories played a critical role in the creation of identities where school achievement and literacy were tied to an individual's identity as an African American.

Counterhegemonic in nature, the school-community operated as an "as-if" community (as if we were free), and it also simultaneously and explicitly recognized the nature of oppression and, as such, mobilized all available resources so that the idea of African Americans as an achieving and a literate people could be realized. The school-community was counterhegemonic in that it acknowledged the nature and extent of the ideological and material oppression of African Americans as students and intentionally organized itself to counter the effects of this oppression. The school-community was counterhegemonic in that it explicitly passed on those dispositions, behaviors, and stances that were viewed as essential to academic achievement (persistence, thoroughness, a desire to do one's very best, commitment to hard work). The school-community was counterhegemonic in that the school's public culture included African-American classical and popular cultural formations, as well as the classical and popular cultural formations of the dominant society. In these schools, indigenous African-American cultural formations were rendered classical, and mainstream classical formations became indigenous.

To call the historically Black schools an imaginary universe is not to imply that it is an individual creation that exists only in someone's head. Figured universes are intentional, imagined, historically contingent, and collectively constituted. These school-communities were organized as if the community of African Americans were free and its members full citizens. At the same time these intentional communities incorporated practices and behaviors that would be expected of African Americans in the larger world, if they were free. Central to a figured universe is a system of symbols, rituals, cultural resources, and cultural artifacts.

In Black churches in the South, it was a common practice to recognize the academic accomplishments of students throughout their academic career. A friend of mine from Prince Edwards County, Virginia, tells the story of how, when he and others would come home from college, the older women in the church would engage in a practice called "palming." Cupping their hand, each woman in the church would put her hand in his hand and give him a dollar or whatever she had, telling him to keep on moving on to higher ground.

Again the central meaning system that becomes concretized, symbolized, and reproduced in the figured universe of the historical Black school is that education is pursued because this is how African Americans affirm their humanity. It is how African Americans assert their identity as a free people. One uplifts the race and prepares oneself to lead one's people by means of education.

What is important here is that this meaning system, this philosophy, which becomes institutionalized, is one that ties the identity of African Americans as a free people to academic achievement. It is then no accident that this philosophy is as powerful as it is, that it has the capacity to create, to develop, and to sustain the desire to achieve in African Americans across generations. This figured universe creates an identity for African Americans, as individuals and as a people, that is not only not at odds with but coincident with intellectual achievement.

How does this meaning system, this theory of education develop? As illustrated earlier, it is not a figment of somebody's imagination at this point and time, somebody who wants to read something into Black institutions, who has nostalgia for them. This philosophy of education emerges out of limitations, out of constraints, out of the struggle for education, and out of the lived experiences of African Americans. The narrative of Frederick Douglass and his interaction with his master and mistress who forbade him from learning how to read and write captures this improvisational form. This story is emblematic of the kind of interactions that took place throughout the slave South and would continue in different forms even after emancipation—precisely because the limitations and the denial of educational opportunity was so unrelenting—up through the Civil Rights era.

THINKING ABOUT AFRICAN-AMERICAN SCHOOL
ACHIEVEMENT IN THE POST–CIVIL RIGHTS ERA

In the post–Civil Rights era, the task of achievement for African-American youth is much more complicated. The idea of African Americans' intellectual inferiority still exists as part of the "taken-for-granted notions" of many people in the larger society, irrespective of political orientation. But at the same time there is the illusion of openness and opportunity.

A twenty-something Black woman who recently completed a Ph.D. from a competitive university was telling me why she really liked one of her professors. She said, "He is one of the few, no, maybe the only white professor I have had during my doctoral studies who didn't automatically assume that because I was Black I was less than competent." A seventeen-year-old female, who has participated in a city-to-suburb busing program since she was five years old, commented, "My teachers always tell me I am so smart, that I am not like the other Black students. They think that this is a compliment, that it will make me feel good. They don't know that it would only make me feel good if I didn't identify with my community, with Black people. Instead it lets me know that they think Black people as a whole are dumb. Every time they make statements like this, I feel bad about myself."

Today, the ideology of Black intellectual inferiority is expressed not only in these kinds of interactions, but also vividly and constantly and with considerable force in the media, which inserts itself into all aspects of our lives. The ideology of African-American inferiority is perhaps more robust today, in terms of its impact on students, than it was in the pre–Civil Rights era. In the pre–Civil Rights era, African-American children and youth lived in communities, attended schools and churches, and were members of organizations that, in response to the larger society's explicit ideology about African Americans' intellectual competence, communicated a counternarrative about their intellectual capacity. Today, few individuals, organizations, and institutions acknowledge or pay attention to the reproduction of the ideology of Black inferiority and its potential impact on African-American students. After all, we live in the post–Civil Rights era. The society is now open. Few respectable people will publicly assert that Black people are intellectually inferior. The visible, in-your-face manifestations of oppression have been mostly eliminated. But you scarcely can find a Black student who cannot recall or give you a litany of instances when he or she was automatically assumed to be intellectually incompetent.

Some years ago, at a competitive university, Black students called having a white professor giving them a grade lower than they deserved "grade bashing." At another competitive university, Black students termed a "B" "the Black B," the grade that in their estimation they would inevitably receive regardless of the quality of their work. It is interesting that these students had developed a language to describe the practices that they thought resulted from their teachers' assessment of them as intellectually inferior. But these are older students who have made it to college. Most seriously African-American children go to K–12 schools in the post–Civil Rights era with little acknowledgment by teachers, administrators, and parents that they are being battered at every turn by the ideology of African-American inferiority. And if the presence of this ideology is acknowledged, usually little or nothing is done to buffer students from impact of this ideology and to develop in students the capacity to resist these assessments. An Asian-American student who had recently finished her student teaching in a K–1 class in the Northeast related to me the remarks her white supervising teacher had made to her predominantly Black class on the occasion that money was missing in the class. The teacher looked directly at the Black students in her class and, in an accusatory manner, told them that they would go to jail if they were caught stealing. A couple of days later, it was discovered that the only two white boys in the class were the ones who had taken the money. A couple of weeks later the student teacher and her teacher found out that the mother of one of the girls whom the teacher had fixed her eyes on when she gave the group of Black children the ominous warning about jail was actually in jail. Upon finding this out, the student teacher asked the teacher, "How do you think your remarks affected Gloria?" According to the student teacher, the teacher was rather nonchalant in her reaction to this question. The student teacher also told me that this same teacher said to her K–1 students, "You are not all going to college, you know, and that is all right. Everybody does not have to go to college."

To further complicate matters, in the post–Civil Rights era, in the mainstream media, the prevailing narrative about schooling is the "narrative of openness and educational opportunity." Newspapers, magazines, and television pass on and reinforce this narrative through the many stories that chronicle the extraordinary school achievement of immigrants of color, particularly Asian Americans. The subtext is "you can make it if you try." After all, Asian Americans have come to this country, and in face of significant hardships, they have succeeded, not only in school but also in the economy. The unarticulated message is that African-American students don't succeed because they are intellectually incompetent or culturally inferior. In Spike Lee's movie *Do the Right Thing,* ML, one of the Black men featured, uses the comedic to capture the irony of this assessment. ML says, "Either dem Koreans are geniuses or we Blacks are dumb." In some urban public school systems and schools in the Northeast, where the student population is predominately people of color, some evidence suggests that a system of stratification is developing among people of color, with African-American students invariably at the bottom. In some of these schools, the ideology of African-American intellectual and cultural inferiority is communicated not only by the behaviors and practices of the teachers, but also by immigrants and their parents, even Black immigrants.

In the post–Civil Rights era, many public schools have become deritualized institutions. Regular assemblies, which were once common in virtually all segregated Black schools and still are at Morehouse College and many historically Black colleges and independent schools, are held at few public schools. Most schools are simply an assemblage of disconnected activities and events. Almost none have a well-articulated message about the intellectual competence of their students. And if a school does have a message, it is often nothing more than a series of statements made by teachers and principals. Few administrators know how to effectively use the cultural formations of their schools' multiracial and multiethnic students to frame a central message, to create a figured community, and to carefully craft a school culture of achievement that has salience for the students.

Coincident with the prevailing "narrative of openness and educational opportunity" is the absence of a conversation about African-American school achievement that is predicated on and that foregrounds the identity of African Americans as African Americans. The conversation about Black achievement often proceeds from the assumption that what is good for one group of children is good for another—unless the distinguishing characteristics are "urban and poor"—categories that are intrinsically ahistoric. The conversation about Black education, when it does occur, and when the controlling categories are "urban" or "poor," usually centers on grade-level performance rather than high academic achievement. The dominant group tends to lead this conversation with African Americans participating at the margins or on the terms of the prevailing discourse. Thus it is no surprise that schools are not organized as intentional, counter-hegemonic communities and that there is an absence of spaces or programs in predominantly white or multiracial institutions that are organized to forge the identities of African-American students as achievers, literate, and a people with a rich intellectual tradition. In the post–Civil Rights era, the school is usually conceptualized singularly as an educational institution, failing to understand that for school to be a powerful institution for African Americans, it must also function as a cultural, social, and political institution.

I would contend that the task of achievement for African-Americans in the post–Civil Rights era is more complicated for the following reasons:

- Schools or spaces in schools are not intentionally organized to forge identities of African-American students as achievers.
- Schools provide few spaces that are intentionally designed to buffer African-American students from the day-to-day experience of racism in the school, and from the explicit and subtle impact of the ideology of Black intellectual inferiority.
- Schools are not likely to have a narrative that is counter to the "narrative of openness and opportunity," one that talks about Black achievement in the face of constraints and limits.
- Schools make few attempts to systematically organize occasions to create desire, to inspire hope, to develop and sustain effort opti-

mism, or to intentionally create multiple contexts that socialize students to the behaviors that are necessary for them to be
achievers.

- There is a conspiracy of silence about how racism in and out of
school blunts effort optimism.
- African-American parents, as the first generation of African-
Americans to experience racism and its impact on achievement in
an allegedly "open and integrated" society, might possibly not
have figured out how to develop institutional formations and pass
on psychological coping strategies to their children that respond to
this new context.

IMPLICATIONS FOR PRACTICE

In light of the aforementioned conversation, what then should
schools, communities, and parents do to promote African-American
school achievement in the post–Civil Rights era?

If we agree with Holland that "identities are the stories we tell
ourselves and the world about who we are, and our attempts to live in
accordance with these stories," the most important thing schools,
families, and communities can do is to figure out how to develop
among African-American children and youth *identities of achievement*.
And social identities are constructed in groups. Although there are
obviously things that parents can do to help their children develop
identities of achievement, the most powerful location for this work is
in the context of the peer group. When school communities are constructed such that membership in these communities means being an
achiever, African-American students achieve in these school communities. Thus African-American youth achieve in Department of Defense schools, in Catholic schools, in some independent schools, in
historically Black colleges, and in white colleges when they participate in programs that intentionally craft a social identity for them as
achievers. Even in schools that are neither responsive to nor pay attention to African-American culture, if the entire school community is
organized around a culture of achievement, if the culture is sufficiently strong, and if African-American students are seen as full members of these communities, these schools seem to be able to counter
the larger society's ideology about the intellectual incompetence of

African Americans. I would speculate that this would be the case even if African-American students encounter individual teachers at these schools, which will almost certainly be the case, who do not see them as intellectually competent.

Community-based programs, churches, and schools must figure out how to deliberately pass on to African-American youth the African-American philosophy of schooling. Not only have I heard white people wish that African Americans valued education as much as immigrants do, but I have also heard African Americans themselves say that we should be like the Jews or Asian Americans and have schools on Saturday for our children. I usually respond by saying that we should be like ourselves and have schools in the evening, on Saturday, or on Sunday, like we did when we ran native schools, Sabbath schools, penny schools, and freedom schools. Intentionally passing on to the next generation the African-American philosophy of education will obviously require studying the history of African-American education and becoming familiar with the African-American narrative tradition and African-American children's literature that reflects this philosophy. This is big, as we have a whole generation of teachers, Black and white, who don't have a clue about the history of Black education and the African-American narrative and intellectual tradition. In Waters's (1999) study, Black immigrants clearly saw themselves as valuing education and Africans Americans as not valuing education. When Waters asked African Americans about what their core values were, they said family and education. Waters seems to suggest that African Americans were tentative about these assertions, since they knew that this is not what the larger society or Black immigrants thought about them. Reenergizing and passing on to the next generation of African-American children the African-American philosophy of education is essential.

Schools, community-based organizations, churches, and groups of families need to create multiple social contexts for African-American youth where being African American is coincident with doing intellectual work and being an achiever. In the school, church, or community-based organization, this could involve organizing ongoing group activities for African-American youth that are intellectual in nature, including film clubs, literary societies, study groups, debating clubs, moot court competitions, African-American history and culture clubs, prelaw societies, and so on. A recent *Boston Globe* article described the Du Bois Society, started by local educational leader and activist Jackie Rivers for Black high school students who were enrolled in competitive or independent high schools. "This self-styled 'honors society' drawing about 35 teenagers from Boston, Cambridge, Belmont, and other communities . . . and meeting weekly at Harvard University and the Baker House . . . , seeks to give Black students a counterweight to what they see as the pressure to . . . shrug off homework and avoid looking white, and to disdain exams as just another imposition by older, white authority figures." In talking to Jackie and her husband, it was clear what their intentions were: they created a social context that affirmed that being Black was coincident with being an achiever, an intellectual. I reminded her that over a decade earlier, another Boston African-American educator and activist, Renee Neblet, had started the African-American History and Culture Club, and for four years, every Saturday my daughter attended this club. African-American scholars and activists, as with the Du Bois Society, also gave lectures to them. The students produced a newspaper, had discussions, and, most important, began to understand that their social identity as African Americans was compatible with being intellectuals. A word about these social group activities— they won't have the power they should unless (a) there is an established protocol for the clubs; (b) they are systematically used to require, to have students practice, and to be the context for the socialization of these young people to the behaviors and practices that are necessary for them to be achievers—persistence, hard work, a commitment to thoroughness and to doing ones' best, and so on; (c) these clubs embody meaningful rituals and symbols that draw on the cultural formations of the students and their communities.

School administrators, parents, community leaders, and teachers will need to create an external review process for schools whereby the school is assessed both for how it reproduces explicitly or in subtle ways the ideology of African-American intellectual inferiority and for how it might, within the context of the school's culture, proactively work to create identities of achievement among African-American students. The Multicultural Assessment Plan, developed and used by the Association of Independent Schools, could serve as a model, not in terms of its content, but in terms of how it is organized and implemented, for school communities interested in moving in this direction. I believe that the Multicultural Assessment Plan has been central in the commitment and progress that some independent schools in the Northeast have made in helping their schools become better places for students of color.

It is extremely important for schools, community-based organizations, and churches to create multiple occasions and contexts in which biculturality and fluency both in African-American language, formal and informal, and standard English, and in African-American popular and classical culture and the culture of power are normalized and are seen as complementary rather than oppositional. Some examples of how this might be accomplished include having oratory contests; inviting as guest lecturers African-American scholars who are excellent speakers precisely because they are fluent in African-American language and standard English; providing regular occasions when students read literature in which the authors demonstrate fluency in both the standard English and African-American language; and, perhaps most important, helping teachers and administrators understand that fluency in cultural formations of African Americans is compatible with the acquisition of cultural capital.

Schools, churches, and community-based organizations need to make sure that the lack of cultural capital is not the reason for the assessment of African-American children as special needs cases. These entities also need to commit themselves to explicitly handing over cultural capital to African-American students, and doing so in such a way that respects and affirms African-American cultural formations.

If African-American children and youth are to achieve at high levels and be able to see and experience themselves as intellectually competent, they need an intellectually challenging curriculum. To tell students that they are smart and to repeatedly teach content that is not intellectually challenging affirms that in reality the students are not seen as smart or intellectually capable.

Racial socialization of African-American children needs to become part of the explicit agenda of parents, community based organizations, and churches. In *Overcoming the Odds: Raising Academically Successful African American Young Women,* Freeman Hrabowski and his colleagues found that college women's parents prepared them to deal with racism and other obstacles that they were likely to face in school because they were Black. According to the authors, "The most common refrain from the fathers to their daughters . . . was that they were as good as anyone else . . . , that they would have to work harder to get ahead . . . , and that the playing field was not always fair. . . . Some fathers (side by side with the mothers) delivered the message before racially charged events occurred. Others responded to the issues as their daughters were confronted by them" (Hrabowski et al. 2002, 76).

African-American families, community-based organizations, and churches need to create a parallel system of schools for African-American children and youth, which would meet on Saturday and weekdays after school. These schools could be the context for supplementary instruction in language arts, literature, and math; the intentional passing on of the African-American philosophy of education; and the education of African-American youth about African-American studies. The scholarship in African-American studies is extensive, but it almost never reaches African-American students enrolled in public or independent schools. There are also many individuals with considerable expertise in curriculum and pedagogy. If our forefathers and foremothers could organize a system of native schools and Sabbath schools, then surely we can do this and more.

TOWARD A THEORY OF
AFRICAN-AMERICAN ACHIEVEMENT

In order for African-American children to achieve in school, they have to be able to negotiate three distinct social identities: their identity as members of a castelike group, their identity as members of mainstream society, and their identity as members of a cultural group in opposition to which whiteness historically and contemporarily continues to be defined.* Given the sociopolitical arrangements of the larger society, these identities are often seen and experienced as contradictory and oppositional to each other. African-American youth

---

*I am drawing on and revising the work of Boykin and Toms (1985), who contend that in order to move toward adult competence African-American children have to acquire competence, negotiating the demands of three distinct and conflicting "arenas of experience, three distinct realms of social negotiation . . . mainstream, minority, and Black cultural" (46). I have tried to historicize the contributions of Boykin and Toms and to focus on social identity rather than realms of experience.

have to be capable of dealing with the dilemmas that emerge from the socially constructed contradictory nature of these identities, as well as those inherent in the identities themselves.

Being a member of a racial caste group automatically brings with it some challenges, in terms of making an ongoing commitment to achievement. These challenges are heightened and particularized for African Americans. For members of a castelike racial minority, the lack of a predictable and comparable relationship between the education and rewards in the marketplace over generations does influence effort optimism, particularly if one's view of schooling and education is primarily instrumental.

But the issues involved in African Americans being able to commit themselves over time to do intellectual work at a high level are also fundamentally informed by the larger society's ideology of African-American intellectual inferiority. For no American group has there been such a persistent, well-articulated, and unabated ideology about their mental incompetence. Thus both African Americans' castelike status and the larger society's ideology about their intellectual competence creates a distinctive set of dilemmas for African-American youth and even adults. African Americans have to develop social, psychological, and political competencies to deal with these dilemmas if they are to commit themselves to doing work that involves the life of the mind.

The African-American theory of knowledge and philosophy of education, which emerged from and was grounded in the lived experience of African Americans, and which has received new articulations over time, has historically been able to provide answers to these very real dilemmas. More specifically, the philosophy of freedom for literacy and literacy for freedom linked literacy and education to the social identity of African Americans, to the very notion of what it meant to be African American, and to African Americans' struggle and yearnings for freedom. With this philosophy of education, schooling was not primarily linked to rewards in the labor market. It was transcendent and powerful enough to sustain the desire to achieve in African Americans, across generations, even when schooling did not result in rewards in the job market. It was also generative of a collective counternarrative, institutionalized and passed on across many generations.

Simultaneously negotiating one's identity as a member of a castelike group and one's identity as a putative member of mainstream society is a balancing act fraught with its own set of dilemmas. In order to achieve in this society, one must maintain the possibility of full membership in American society. At the same time, as a member of a racial caste group, one has to have an interpretive framework that is capable of making sense of those instances when effort does not lead to comparable rewards, when one experiences discrimination in school and in the larger society. As a student of mine reflected on what it takes for African-American students to achieve in school, she said, "You have to work as if the society were open but accept the fact that because you are Black, sometimes it will be closed." In other words, for African-American students to achieve, they need to be sufficiently grounded in their identity as members of a racial caste group, such that they have a way to interpret and make sense of instances when they experience discrimination, especially in school. If children are not grounded in this way, they would likely blame themselves when their work is not recognized or not evaluated fairly. On the other hand, if children pay too much attention to their status as members of a racially discriminated group, there might be a tendency not to work hard, not to work as if the society were open. As is quite apparent, balancing these two identities requires the development of psychosocial competencies, as well as explicit racial socialization by the family, church, or community-based organization.

Negotiating identity as a member of a cultural group in opposition to which whiteness has been defined is equally problematic. The cultural formations of African Americans, particularly language, lead people to make judgments about the intellectual competence of African Americans. At the same time the schizophrenic reactions of Americans to these cultural formations and the high-profile way people from all walks of life consume African-American culture creates dilemmas. It is particularly hard to explain to a Black youth why the Black aesthetic, expressed in the Black body, puts off members of the dominant society, who at the same time use African-American cultural formations for everything from the marketing of Wall Street products to the selling of Coca-Cola. Furthermore, it is hard to explain to a Black youth why individuals make judgments about him and his intellectual competence when he wears hip-hop gear and yet don't make similar judgments about the average white boy from suburbia, headed to Brown or Harvard, who wears these clothes.

Simultaneously negotiating one's identity as a member of mainstream society and as a member of a cultural group also creates dilemmas, given the oppositional nature of these identities in the American imagination. Commitment to achievement requires not only that one hold open the possibility of full participation in mainstream society, but also that one possess and commit to acquiring cultural capital. And one has to consent to the acquisition of cultural capital, even as one understands that cultural capital is often viewed as oppositional to African-American cultural formations, which are seen as inferior when represented in the Black body.

Given the above, what predictions can we make about the kind of environments that are likely to promote or impede academic achievement among African Americans? African-American students will achieve in school environments that have a leveling culture, a culture of achievement that extends to all of its members and a strong sense of group membership, where the expectation that everyone achieve is explicit and is regularly communicated in public and group settings. African-American students will achieve in these environments, irrespective of class background, the cultural responsiveness of the setting, or prior level of preparation. Thus we can understand why it is that African-American students achieve in Department of Defense schools, in Catholic schools, in Black colleges, in independent schools, and in the Prescott Elementary School in Oakland. In addition to having the aforementioned characteristics, institutions that are culturally responsive and that systematically affirm, draw on, and use cultural formations of African Americans will produce *exceptional academic results* from African-American students. Usually in these school communities, there are academic support services available to ensure that all students are able to achieve, as well as a determination to socialize students to the behaviors and values that support achievement.

African-American students will have difficulty achieving in school communities, irrespective of class background and prior level of academic preparation, that are individualistic, committed to giving their students lots of degrees of freedom, and highly stratified and competitive and that make few attempts to build and ritualize a common, strong culture of achievement that extends to all students.

Schools in this category include many of the highly ranked systems in small towns, progressive college towns, and suburban communities. Schools in progressive college towns have the added burden of having an explicit and strong narrative about equality, an institutionalized system of stratification, and in many instances an even greater commitment to individual freedom than schools in small towns and suburban communities. If educators and parents are able to organize social and cultural groups designed to forge identities of achievement, groups that are the context for a range of academic activities, from study groups to speaker series, and that help students acquire those behaviors that are necessary for them to be achievers, then African-American students will be able to achieve in these kinds of school communities.

STEREOTYPE THREAT AND AFRICAN-AMERICAN STUDENT ACHIEVEMENT

The buildings had hardly changed in the thirty years since I'd been to the small liberal arts school quite near the college that I attended. In my student days I had visited it many times to see friends. This time I was there to give a speech about how racial and gender stereotypes, floating and abstract though they might seem, can affect concrete things like grades, test scores, and academic identity. My talk was received warmly, and the next morning I met with a small group of African-American students. I have done this on many campuses. But this time, perhaps cued by the familiarity of the place, I had an experience of déjà vu. The students expressed a litany of complaints that could have come straight from the mouths of the Black friends I had visited there thirty years earlier: the curriculum was too white, they heard too little Black music, they were ignored in class, and too often they felt slighted by faculty members and other students. Despite the school's recruitment efforts, they were a small minority. The core of their social life was their own group. To relieve the dysphoria, they went home a lot on weekends.

I found myself giving them the same advice my father gave me when I was in college: lighten up on the politics, get the best education you can, and move on. But then I surprised myself by saying, "To do this you have to learn from people who part of yourself tells you are difficult to trust."

Over the past four decades African-American college students have been more in the spotlight than any other American students. This is because they aren't just college students; they are a cutting edge in America's effort to integrate itself in the nearly forty years since the passage of the Civil Rights Act. These students have borne much of the burden for our national experiment in racial integration. And to a significant degree the success of the experiment will be determined by their success.

Nonetheless, throughout the 1990s the national college dropout rate for African Americans has been 20 to 25 percent higher than that for whites. Among those who finish college, the grade point average of Black students is two-thirds of a grade below that of whites.

A recent study by William Bowen and Derek Bok, reported in their book *The Shape of the River* (1998), brings some happy news: despite this underachievement in college, Black students who attend the most selective schools in the country go on to do just as well in postgraduate programs and professional attainment as other students from those schools. This is a telling fact in support of affirmative action, since only these schools use affirmative action in admissions. Still, the underperformance of Black undergraduates is an unsettling problem, one that may alter or hamper career development, especially among Blacks not attending the most selective schools.

Attempts to explain the problem can sound like a debate about whether America is a good society, at least by the standard of racial fairness, and maybe even about whether racial integration is possible. It is an uncomfortably finger-pointing debate. Does the problem stem from something about Black students themselves, such as poor motivation, a distracting peer culture, lack of family values, or—the unsettling suggestion of *The Bell Curve*—genes? Or does it stem from the conditions of Blacks' lives: social and economic deprivation, a society that views Blacks through the lens of diminishing stereotypes and low expectations, too much coddling, or too much neglect?

In recent years this debate has acquired a finer focus: the fate of middle-class Black students. Americans have come to view the disadvantages associated with being Black as disadvantages primarily of social and economic resources and opportunity. This assumption is often taken to imply that if you are Black and come from a socioeconomically middle-class home, you no longer suffer a significant disadvantage of race. "Why should the son of a Black physician be given an advantage in college admission over the son of a white delivery-truck driver?" This is a standard question in the controversy over affirmative action. And the assumption behind it is that surely in today's society the disadvantages of race are overcome when lower socioeconomic status is overcome.

But virtually all aspects of underperformance—lower standardized test scores, lower college grades, lower graduation rates—persist among students from the African-American middle class. This situation forces on us an uncomfortable recognition: that beyond class, something racial is depressing the academic performance of these students.

Some time ago two of my colleagues, Joshua Aronson and Steven Spencer, and I tried to see the world from the standpoint of these students, concerning ourselves less with features of theirs that might explain their troubles than with features of the world they see. A story I was told recently depicts some of these. The storyteller was worried about his friend, a normally energetic Black student who had broken up with his longtime girlfriend and had since learned that she, a Hispanic, was now dating a white student. This hit him hard. Not long after hearing about his girlfriend, he sat through an hour's discussion of *The Bell Curve* in his psychology class, during which the possible genetic inferiority of his race was openly considered. Then he overheard students at lunch arguing that affirmative action allowed in too many underqualified Blacks. By his own account, this young man had experienced very little of what he thought of as racial discrimination on campus. Still, these were features of his world. Could they have a bearing on his academic life?

My colleagues and I have called such features "stereotype threat"—the threat of being viewed through the lens of a negative stereotype, or the fear of doing something that would inadvertently confirm that stereotype. Everyone experiences stereotype threat. We are all members of some group about which negative stereotypes exist, from white males and Methodists to women and the elderly. And in a situation where one of those stereotypes applies—a man talking to women about pay equity, for example, or an aging faculty member trying to remember a number sequence in the middle of a lecture—we know that we may be judged by it.

Like the young man in the story, we can feel mistrustful and apprehensive in such situations. For him, as for African-American students generally, negative stereotypes apply in many situations, even personal ones. Why was that old roommate unfriendly to him? Did that young white woman who has been so nice to him in class not return his phone call because she's afraid he'll ask her for a date? Is it because of his race or something else about him? He cannot know the answers, but neither can his rational self fully dismiss the questions. Together they raise a deeper question: Will his race be a boundary to his experience, to his emotions, to his relationships?

Consider the experience that Brent Staples, now an editorialist for the *New York Times,* recounted in his autobiography, *Parallel Time* (1994). When he arrived at the University of Chicago's Hyde Park campus to begin graduate school in psychology, he noticed that as an African-American male dressed like a student, he seemed to make people apprehensive; on the street people seemed to avoid him, in shops security people followed him, and so on. After a while he realized that he was being seen through the lens of a negative stereotype about his race. It wasn't that he had done anything to warrant this view of him—as in taking too much food, for example. It was simply that he was an identifiable member of a group about whom existed a broadly held negative view of their proneness to violence. Moreover, walking the streets of Hyde Park, he was in a situation where this negative view was applicable to him—every time he was in the setting. Thus this stereotype confronted him with an engulfing predicament. It was relevant to a broad range of behaviors in the setting—just walking down the street or entering a store, for example, could be seen by others through the lens of the stereotype as foreshadowing danger. Also, everyone in his environment knows the stereotype. Thus it could influence and coordinate how he was judged and treated by many people. And it would be difficult for him to prove to people, on the spot, that this view of his group was not applicable to him as a person. In these ways, then, the threat posed by this group stereotype becomes a formidable predicament, one that could make it difficult for him to trust that he would be seen objectively and treated with good will in the setting. Such, then, is the hypothesized nature of stereotype threat—not an abstract threat, not necessarily a belief or expectation about oneself, but the concrete, real-time threat of being judged and treated poorly in settings where a negative stereotype about one's group applies.

MEASURING STEREOTYPE THREAT

Can stereotype threat be shown to affect academic performance? And if so, who would be most affected—stronger or weaker students? Which has a greater influence on academic success among Black college students—the degree of threat or the level of preparation with which they enter college? Can the college or other educational experience be redesigned to lessen the threat? And if so, would that redesign help these students to succeed academically?

As we confronted these questions in the course of our research, we came in for some surprises. We began with what we took to be the hardest question: Could something as abstract as stereotype threat really affect something as irrepressible as intelligence? Ours is an individualistic culture; forward movement is seen to come from within. Against this cultural faith one needs evidence to argue that something as "sociological" as stereotype threat can repress something as "individualistic" as intelligence.

To acquire such evidence, Joshua Aronson and I (following a procedure developed with Steven Spencer) designed an experiment to test whether the stereotype threat that Black students might experience when taking a difficult standardized test could depress their performance on the test to a statistically reliable degree. We brought white and Black Stanford students into the laboratory and gave them, one at a time, a very difficult thirty-minute section of a Graduate Record Exam subject test in English literature. Most of these students were sophomores, which meant that the test—designed for graduating seniors—was particularly hard for them—precisely the feature, we reasoned, that would make this simple testing situation different for our Black participants than for our white participants, despite the fact that all the participants were of equal ability levels measured by all available criteria. (The difficulty of the test guaranteed that both Black and white students would find the test frustrating. And it is in these situations that members of ability-stereotyped groups are most likely to experience the extra burden of stereotype threat. First, the experience of frustration with the test gives credibility to the limitation alleged in the stereotype. For this reason, frustration can be especially stinging and disruptive for test-takers to whom the stereotype is relevant. Second, it is on a demanding test that one can least afford to be bothered by the thoughts that likely accompany stereotype threat.)

A significant part of the negative stereotype about African Americans concerns intellectual ability. Thus, in the stereotype threat conditions of the experiments in this series, we merely mentioned to participants that the test was a measure of verbal ability. This was enough, we felt, to make the negative stereotype about African Americans' abilities relevant to their performance on the test, and thus to put them at risk of confirming, or being seen to confirm, the negative stereotype about their abilities. If the pressure imposed by the relevance of a negative stereotype about one's group is enough to impair an important intellectual performance, then Black participants should perform worse than whites in the "diagnostic" condition of this experiment but not in the "nondiagnostic" condition. As figure 1 depicts, this is precisely what happened: Blacks performed a full standard deviation lower than whites under the stereotype threat of the test being "diagnostic" of their intellectual ability, even though we had statistically matched the two groups in ability level. Something other than ability was involved; we believed it was stereotype threat.

But maybe the Black students performed less well than the white students because they were less motivated, or because their skills were somehow less applicable to the advanced material of this test. We needed some way to determine if it was indeed stereotype threat that depressed the Black students' scores. We reasoned that if stereotype threat had impaired their performance on the test, then reducing this threat would allow their performance to improve. We presented the same test as a laboratory task that was used to study how certain problems are generally solved. We stressed that the task did not measure a person's level of intellectual ability. A simple instruction, yes, but it profoundly changed the meaning of the situation. In one stroke "spotlight anxiety," as the psychologist William Cross once called it, was turned off—and the Black students' performance on the test rose to match that of equally qualified whites (see figure 1). In the nonstereotype threat conditions, we presented the same test as an instrument for studying problem solving that was "nondiagnostic" of individual differences in ability—thus making the racial stereotype irrelevant to their performance.

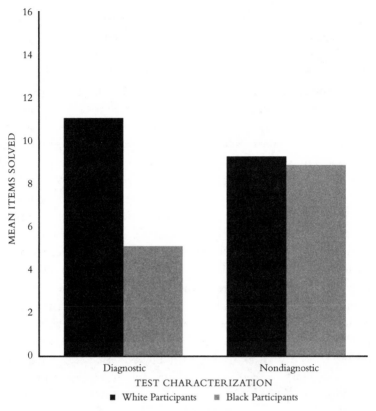

Figure 1. White and Black participants' score (controlled for SAT) on a difficult English test as a function of characterization of the test.

Aronson and I decided that what we needed next was direct evidence of the subjective state we call stereotype threat. To seek this, we looked into whether simply sitting down to take a difficult test of ability was enough to make Black students mindful of their race and stereotypes about it. This may seem unlikely. White students I have taught over the years have sometimes said that they have hardly any sense of even having a race. But Blacks have many experiences with the majority "other group" that make their race salient to them.

We again brought Black and white students in to take a difficult verbal test. But just before the test began, we gave them a long list of words, each of which had two letters missing. They were told to complete the words on this list as fast as they could. We knew from a preliminary survey that twelve of the eighty words we had selected could be completed in such a way as to relate to the stereotype about Blacks' intellectual ability. The fragment "—ce," for example, could become "race." If simply taking a difficult test of ability was enough to make Black students mindful of stereotypes about their race, these students should complete more fragments with stereotype-related words. That is just what happened. When Black students were told that the test would measure ability, they completed the fragments with significantly more stereotype-related words than when they were told that it was not a measure of ability. Whites made few stereotype-related completions in either case.

What kind of worry is signaled by this race consciousness? To find out, we used another probe. We asked participants on the brink of the difficult test to tell us their preferences in sports and music. Some of these, such as basketball, jazz, and hip-hop, are associated with African-American imagery, whereas others, such as tennis, swimming, and classical music, are not. Something striking emerged: when Black students expected to take a test of ability, they spurned things African-American, reporting less interest in, for instance, basketball, jazz, and hip-hop than whites did. When the test was presented as unrelated to ability, Black students strongly preferred things African-American. They eschewed these things only when preferring them would encourage a stereotypic view of themselves. It was the spotlight that they were trying to avoid.

Another question arises: Do the effects of stereotype threat come entirely from the fear of being stereotyped, or do they come from something internal to Black students—self-doubt, for example?

Beginning with George Herbert Mead's idea of the "looking-glass self," social psychology has assumed that one's self-image derives in large part from how one is viewed by others—family, school, and the broader society. When those views are negative, people may internalize them, resulting in lower self-esteem—or self-hatred, as it has been called. This theory was first applied to the experience of Jews, by Sigmund Freud and Bruno Bettelheim, but it was also soon applied to the experience of African Americans, by Gordon Allport, Frantz Fanon, Kenneth Clark, and others. According to the theory, Black students internalize negative stereotypes as performance anxiety and low expectations for achievement, which they then fulfill. The "self-fulfilling prophecy" has become a commonplace about these students. Stereotype threat, however, is something different, something external: the situational threat of being negatively stereotyped. Which of these two processes, then, caused the results of our experiments?

Joshua Aronson, Michael Lustina, Kelli Keough, Joseph Brown, Catherine Good, and I devised a way to find out. Suppose we told white male students who were strong in math that a difficult math test they were about to take was one on which Asians generally did better than whites. White males should not have a sense of group inferiority about math, since no societal stereotype alleges such an inferiority. Yet this comment would put them under a form of stereotype threat: any faltering on the test could cause them to be seen negatively from the standpoint of the positive stereotype about Asians and math ability. If stereotype threat alone—in the absence of any internalized self-doubt—was capable of disrupting test performance, then white males taking the test after this comment should perform less well than white males taking the test without hearing the comment. That is just what happened. Stereotype threat impaired intellectual functioning in a group unlikely to have any sense of group inferiority (Aronson et al. 1999).

In science, as in the rest of life, few things are definitive. But these results are pretty good evidence that stereotype threat's impairment of standardized-test performance does not depend on cueing a preexisting anxiety. Steven Spencer, Diane Quinn, and I have shown how stereotype threat depresses the performance of accomplished female math students on a difficult math test, and how that performance improves dramatically when the threat is lifted (Spencer, Steele, and Quinn 1999).

We recruited women and men students at the University of Michigan who were quite good at math—with entering math SAT scores in the top 15 percent of the Michigan student population—and who were identified with math in the sense of seeing it as very important to their personal and career goals. We brought them into the laboratory one at a time, and to mimic the condition that seemed to produce women's math underperformance in the real world, we gave all participants a very difficult math test—a twenty-five-minute section of the Graduate Record Exam subject exam in mathematics. The sheer difficulty of the test, we reasoned, would be enough to make the nega-

tive stereotype about women's math ability relevant to them person-
ally, despite their confidence in their mathematical abilities, and thus
to threaten them with the possibility that they would be confirming
the stereotype, or be seen as confirming it. Following our real world
observations, we assumed that nothing more pointed than taking
such a test would be required to evoke this threat, and in turn, this
threat should depress women's performance relative to men's, even
though we had selected men and women who were equally good at
math and cared equally about it.

This is precisely what happened. In one early experiment, women
underperformed in relation to men on a difficult math test but not on
a difficult English test, and in another, women again underperformed
in relation to men on a difficult math test but not on an easier math test
that did not cause the same level of frustration.

With these findings we had produced the same gendered pattern
of behavior that we had observed in the real world of difficult math
classes. But these findings, again, did not establish that it was stereotype threat that was responsible for depressing women's performance
on the difficult test. As was pointed out to us, they could reflect the
fact that women have some lesser capacity specifically for math that
reveals itself only when the math is very difficult. To distinguish between these explanations, we devised a condition in the next experiment, as we did in the experiment with Black and white Stanford
students, that reduced stereotype threat by making the stereotype irrelevant to performance. The test was presented to all participants as
one that did not show sex differences, as a test in which women always
did as well as men—thus making the stereotype about women's math
ability irrelevant to interpreting their experience while taking this
particular test. The results in this condition were dramatic. As figure 2
shows, women given this instruction performed just as well as equally
skilled men and significantly better than women in the stereotype-
still-relevant condition of this experiment in which participants were
told that the test did show gender differences.

The mere relevance of the negative stereotype to their own math
performance, presumably occasioned by their performance frustration, was enough to undermine the test performance of strong
women math students who cared a lot about math. Jean-Claude
Croizet, working in France with a stereotype that links poor verbal

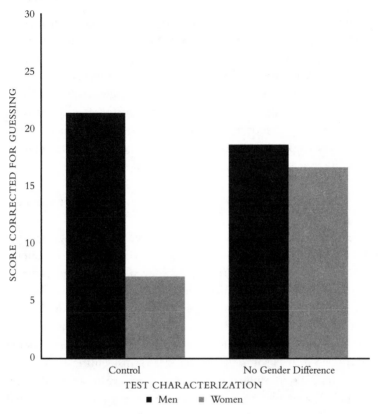

Figure 2. Men's and women's mean score (controlled for guessing) on a difficult math test as a function of characterization of the test.

skills with lower-class status, found analogous results: lower-class college students performed less well than upper-class college students under the threat of a stereotype-based judgment, but performed as well when the threat was removed.

The stereotype threat's impairing effects also generalize to other performance domains. Stone and his colleagues (1999) have established an intriguing effect of stereotype threat on sports performance. They asked elite athletes at the University of Arizona, Black and white, to perform ten holes of golf in a miniature laboratory course. To invoke a stereotype that would put the performance of white athletes under threat, they introduced the task as a measure of "natural athletic ability." Under this representation, one that puts white athletes under the added risk of confirming or being seen to confirm a

negative group stereotype, the white athletes significantly underperformed in comparison with the Black athletes. But Stone et al. were
able to reverse this pattern of results—so that white athletes outper-
formed Black athletes on the same task—by representing the task as a
measure of "sport strategic intelligence," a representation that now
put the performance of Black athletes under the threat of confirming
a negative group stereotype. These results show the group-by-situa-
tion variability of stereotype threat but also suggest its generalizability
in real life across groups, settings, and types of behavior.

HOW STEREOTYPE THREAT AFFECTS PEOPLE DIFFERENTLY

Is everyone equally threatened and disrupted by a stereotype? One
might expect, for example, that it would affect the weakest students
most. But in all our research the most achievement-oriented students,
who were also the most skilled, motivated, and confident, were the
most impaired by stereotype threat. This fact had been under our
noses all along—in our data and even in our theory. A person has to
care about a domain in order to be disturbed by the prospect of being
stereotyped in it. That is the whole idea of disidentification—pro-
tecting against stereotype threat by ceasing to care about the domain
in which the stereotype applies. Our earlier experiments had selected
Black students who identified with verbal skills and women who
identified with math. But when we tested participants who identified
less with these domains, what had been under our noses hit us in the
face. None of them showed any effect of stereotype threat whatsoever.

These weakly identified students did not perform well on the test:
once they discovered its difficulty, they stopped trying very hard and
got a low score. But their performance did not differ depending on
whether they felt they were at risk of being judged stereotypically.

This finding, I believe, tells us two important things. The first is
that the poorer college performance of Black students may have another source in addition to the one—lack of good preparation and,
perhaps, of identification with school achievement—that is commonly understood. This additional source—the threat of being
negatively stereotyped in the environment—has not been well understood. The distinction has important policy implications: different
kinds of students may require different pedagogies of improvement.

The second thing is poignant: what exposes students to the pressure of stereotype threat is not weaker academic identity and skills but stronger academic identity and skills. They may have long seen themselves as good students—better than most. But led into the domain by their strengths, they pay an extra tax on their investment—vigilant worry that their future will be compromised by society's perception and treatment of their group.

This tax has a long tradition in the Black community. The Jackie Robinson story is a central narrative of Black life, literature, and journalism. *Ebony Magazine* has run a page for fifty years featuring people who have broken down one or another racial barrier. Surely the academic vanguard among Black college students today knows this tradition—and knows, therefore, that the thing to do, as my father told me, is to buckle down, pay whatever tax is required, and disprove the damn stereotype.

That, however, seems to be precisely what these students are trying to do. In some of our experiments we administered the test of ability by computer, so that we could see how long participants spent looking at different parts of the test questions. Black students taking the test under stereotype threat seemed to be trying too hard rather than not hard enough. They reread the questions, reread the multiple choices, rechecked their answers, more than when they were not under stereotype threat. The threat made them inefficient on a test that, like most standardized tests, is set up so that thinking long often means thinking wrong, especially on difficult items like the ones we used.

Philip Uri Treisman, an innovator in math workshops for minority students who is based at the University of Texas, saw something similar in his Black calculus students at the University of California at Berkeley: they worked long hours alone, but they worked inefficiently—for example, checking and rechecking their calculations against the correct answers at the back of the book, rather than focusing on the concepts involved. Of course, trying extra hard helps with some school tasks. But under stereotype threat this effort may be misdirected. Achievement at the frontier of one's skills may be furthered more by a relaxed, open concentration than by a strong desire to disprove a stereotype by not making mistakes.

Sadly, the effort that accompanies stereotype threat exacts an additional price. Led by James Blascovich, of the University of California at Santa Barbara, we found that the blood pressure of Black students performing a difficult cognitive task under stereotype threat was elevated compared with that of Black students not under stereotype threat or white students in either situation (Blascovich et al. 2001).

In the old song about the "steel-drivin' man," John Henry races the new steam-driven drill to see who can dig a hole faster. When the race is over, John Henry has prevailed by digging the deeper hole— only to drop dead. The social psychologist Sherman James uses the term "John Henryism" to describe a psychological syndrome that he found to be associated with hypertension in several samples of North Carolina Blacks: holding too rigidly to the faith that discrimination and disadvantage can be overcome with hard work and persistence. Certainly this is the right attitude. But taken to extremes, it can backfire. A deterioration of performance under stereotype threat by the skilled, confident Black students in our experiments may be rooted in John Henryism.

This last point can be disheartening. Our research, however, offers an interesting suggestion about what can be done to overcome stereotype threat and its detrimental effects. The success of Black students may depend less on expectations and motivation—things that are thought to drive academic performance—than on trust that stereotypes about their group will not have a limiting effect in their school world.

Putting this idea to the test, Joseph Brown and I asked, How can the usual detrimental effect of stereotype threat on the standardized-test performance of these students be reduced? By strengthening students' expectations and confidence, or by strengthening their trust that they are not at risk of being judged on the basis of stereotypes? In the ensuing experiment we strengthened or weakened participants' confidence in their verbal skills, by arranging for them to have either an impressive success or an impressive failure on a test of verbal skills, just before they took the same difficult verbal test we had used in our earlier research. When the second test was presented as a test of ability, the boosting or weakening of confidence in their verbal skills had no effect on performance: Black participants performed less well than equally skilled white participants. What does this say about the commonsense idea that black students' academic problems are rooted in lack of self-confidence?

What did raise the level of black students' performance to that of equally qualified whites was reducing stereotype threat—in this case by explicitly presenting the test as racially fair. When this was done, Blacks performed at the same high level as whites even if their self-confidence had been weakened by a prior failure.

These results suggest something that I think has not been made clear elsewhere: when strong Black students sit down to take a difficult standardized test, the extra apprehension they feel in comparison with whites is less about their own ability than it is about having to perform on a test and in a situation that may be primed to treat them stereotypically. We discovered the extent of this apprehension when we tried to develop procedures that would make our Black participants see the test as "race-fair." It wasn't easy. African-Americans have endured so much bad press about test scores for so long that, in our experience, they are instinctively wary about the tests' fairness. We were able to convince them that our test was race-fair only when we implied that the research generating the test had been done by Blacks. When they felt trust, they performed well regardless of whether we had weakened their self-confidence beforehand. And when they didn't feel trust, no amount of bolstering of self-confidence helped.

ACUTE REACTIONS AND CHRONIC ADAPTATIONS TO STEREOTYPE THREAT

A brief word about the reactions—short- and long-term—that stereotype threat elicits. Early on in our research program (Aronson, Quinn, and Spencer 1998; Steele 1992, 1997), we emphasized how stereotype threat can lead people to disidentify with the domains in which they experience the threat. Pain is lessened by ceasing to identify with the part of life in which the pain occurs. This withdrawal of psychic investment may be supported by other members of the stereotype-threatened group—even to the point of its becoming a group norm. But not caring can mean not being motivated. And this can have real costs. When stereotype threat affects school life, disidentification is a high price to pay for psychic comfort. Still, it is a price that groups contending with powerful negative stereotypes about their abilities—women in advanced math, African Americans in all academic areas—may too often pay.

As research on this question has progressed, two things have become clear: First, people's reactions to stereotype threat include both acute protective reactions and chronic identity adaptations, and second, these reactions are remarkably nuanced, in the sense of taking many concrete forms, so that the picture painted in the previous paragraph is only part of the story. The range of reactions—from avoidance, to counterstereotypic behavior, to disengagement, to full disidentification—form a continuum of psychological responses, just now being studied in a rigorous way with controlled experiments. I address these complex issues in much greater depth elsewhere (Steele, Spencer, and Aronson 2002). But one thing one can say is that some of these strategies—however useful psychologically—do have the effect of lowering performance.

Having a social identity that can elicit devaluation in a setting that one wants to belong to causes conflicting motivations of the sort that W. E. B. Du Bois may have had in mind when he described the "double consciousness" inherent in the African-American experience. One is motivated to detect cues signaling identity-based devaluation, and yet one is motivated not to detect them. One becomes sensitive to the very things one least wants to see. The resulting ruminative conflict coupled with the threat of devaluation in the setting stand as ongoing pressures against, at the very least, a full engagement in the setting, and at the most, the ability to endure it at all.

REMEDYING THE DETRIMENTAL EFFECTS
OF STEREOTYPE THREATS

What are some of the remedies that schools and colleges can use to reduce the negative effects of stereotype threat on minority students, and African-American students in particular?

Policies for helping Black students rest in significant part on assumptions about their psychology. Often they are assumed to lack confidence, which spawns a policy of confidence-building. This may be useful for some students. But the psychology of many others, including the best prepared and most committed students, appears different—underperformance appears to be rooted less in self-doubt than in social mistrust.

We have seen that underachievement problems are caused, in

some part, by threat, by persistent patterns of stereotype threat that, as something tied to a person's social identity in school and workplace settings, can become a chronic feature of his or her experience in those settings. Despite the many cues in a setting that can evoke a sense of threat, therefore, a remedial strategy has to somehow refute that threat or its relevance to the target. My colleagues and I have recently called this goal "identity safety" (Markus, Steele, and Steele 2000; Plaut in press; Purdie et al. 2001). To the extent that it is achieved in an academic setting, it should weaken the sequelae of identity vigilance, mistrust, disidentification, and underperformance. So it follows that education policy relevant to non-Asian minorities might fruitfully shift its focus toward fostering identity safety—and its correlate, racial trust—in the schooling situation, at least among students who come to school with good skills and high expectations. But how should this be done?

Identity safety may be easier to achieve than it might seem at first glance. A couple of school-based examples will suggest some fruitful directions. Again, research on how to create identity safety is complex and expanding, and I explore it in much greater depth elsewhere (Steele, Spencer, and Aronson 2002).

Research shows that solutions include strategies at the level of (1) pedagogy and relationships between individual teachers and students; (2) institutional and contextual changes; and (3) individual personal responses.

To explore the relational component, Geoffrey Cohen, Lee Ross, and I took up the question of how a teacher or a mentor could give critical feedback across the "racial divide" and have that feedback be trusted. We reasoned that an answer to this question might yield insights about how to instill trust more broadly in the schooling environment. Cohen's hunch was that niceness alone wouldn't be enough. But the first question had to be whether there was in fact a racial divide between teachers and students, especially in the elite college environment in which we worked.

We set up a simple experiment. Cohen asked Black and white Stanford students one at a time to write essays about their favorite teachers, for possible publication in a journal on teaching. They were asked to return several days later for feedback on their essays. Before each student left the first writing session, Cohen put a Polaroid snapshot of the student on top of his or her essay. His ostensible purpose was to publish the picture if the essay was published. His real purpose was to let the essay writers know that the evaluator of their writing would be aware of their race. When they returned days later, they were given constructive but critical feedback. We looked at whether different ways of giving this feedback engendered different degrees of trust in it.

We found that neither straight feedback nor feedback preceded by the "niceness" of a cushioning statement ("There were many good things about your essay") was trusted by Black students. They saw these criticisms as probably biased, and they were less motivated than white students to improve their essays. White students took the criticism at face value—even as an indication of interest in them. Black students, however, faced a different meaning: the "ambiguating" possibility that the criticism was motivated by negative stereotypes about their group as much as by the work itself. Herein lies the power of race to make one's world insecure—quite apart from whatever actual discrimination one may experience.

But this experiment also revealed a way to be critical across the racial divide: tell the students that you are using high standards (this signals that the criticism reflects standards rather than race), and that your reading of their essays leads you to believe that they can meet those standards (this signals that you do not view them stereotypically). This shouldn't be faked. High standards, at least in a relative sense, should be an inherent part of teaching, and critical feedback should be given in the belief that the recipient can reach those standards. These things go without saying for many students. But they have to be made explicit for students under stereotype threat. The good news of this study is that when they are made explicit, the students trust and respond to criticism. Black students who got this kind of feedback saw it as unbiased and were motivated to take their essays home and work on them even though this was not a class for credit. They were more motivated than any other group of students in the study—as if this combination of high standards and assurance was like water on parched land, a much-needed but seldom-received balm. In a situation that would otherwise cause a trust-breaking social identity threat among Black students—as evidenced by the results in the other feedback conditions—this simple relational strategy of using high standards and ability affirmation was sufficient to completely overcome the mistrust. The entire context did not have to change for trust to be achieved; one stereotype-refuting relational act was enough.

Contextual solutions are themselves possible, and just being explored rigorously in studies. They include direct interventions designed to refute the possibility of the stereotype threat, representing a philosophy and reality of diversity, and demanding fair, procedural justice for all groups. The findings here are complex and evolving (Steele, Spencer, and Aronson 2002). As this research progresses, it will, I believe, be very important for educational policy makers.

Almost invariably when my colleagues and I give talks about stereotype threat and how to reduce it in school or organizational settings, a question arises: "You have a lot to say about how situations and relationships can be changed to preempt or reduce this threat. But what can individuals, the potential targets, do to cope with this threat, to reduce its effect on them?" The answer to this question, from the standpoint of our theory, begins with the same assumption as the other strategies of remedy: to reduce this threat, individuals have to do something that disarms the appraisal hypothesis that they are under threat, or that, if they are, it will significantly affect them.

Influenced by the research of Carol Dweck and her colleagues (c.f. Dweck, Chiu, and Hong 1995), Joshua Aronson, Carrie Fried, and Cathleen Good (2002) tested the hypothesis that a personal theory of intelligence as incremental—the view that one's intelligence is expandable through effort and experience—could reduce the impact of stereotype threat on people whose intellectual abilities are negatively stereotyped. Dweck has distinguished two personal theories about the nature of intelligence, one that assumes intelligence is essentially a fixed entity and the other that assumes it is expandable. Aronson, Fried, and Good reasoned that if the characteristic impugned in a negative stereotype is seen as improvable rather than fixed, then the threat of the stereotype is not as great. Thus, holding the theory that one's intelligence is malleable could be an effective strategy to cope with the threat posed by negative ability stereotypes.

Aronson, Fried, and Good examined whether this strategy could reduce the effect on academic performance of the negative ability stereotypes that African-American students face. To do this, they developed a clever way of manipulating the theory of intelligence held in a sample of Black and white college students. They cast study participants in the role of "long-distance" mentors to individual elementary school students who were ostensibly from disadvantaged backgrounds. The job of the college-aged mentors—done in a single session—was to write letters to the younger mentees urging them to apply themselves to their schoolwork and, in the critical condition, to think of their intelligence as something that was expandable. Ostensibly to make these letters convincing, the college mentors were supplied compelling descriptions of how intelligence, even the brain itself, could be modified and expanded by effort and learning, something, of course, obviously borne out by contemporary psychology and neuroscience.

Of course the focus of this study was not on the young mentees, but on how the experience of having advocated a malleable theory of intelligence affected the mentors themselves. For the Black college-aged mentors, the group whose abilities are presumably under the threat of negative stereotypes about their group, the effect of this manipulation was dramatic. Compared with Black students who did not write a letter, or who wrote a letter without the "malleability" content, Black students who wrote the "malleable" letter believed that intelligence was more malleable, reported enjoying academics more, saw academics as more important, and most dramatically, at the end of the academic quarter, got significantly higher grades.

Here, then, is clear evidence of something an individual can do to reduce the threat posed by negative ability stereotypes: adopt a self theory of intelligence as expandable. Such a theory may foster achievement through multiple effects. But over the long run, we suggest that one of its ingredients is its ability to dampen the threatening meaning of negative stereotypes about intellectual ability. Again, this is one example of an individual strategy. For an exploration of many others, see Steele, Spencer, and Aronson 2002.

A final example set in situ, in the buzz of everyday life, shows that relatively modest interventions to create identity safety in real world settings can have a dramatic effect.

Steven Spencer, P. G. Davies, Kent Harber, Richard Nisbett, and I undertook a program aimed at incoming first-year students at the University of Michigan. Like virtually all other institutions of higher learning, Michigan had evidence of Black students' underachievement. Our mission was clear: to see if we could improve their achievement by focusing on their transition into college life.

We also wanted to see how little we could get away with—that is, to develop a program that would succeed broadly without special efforts. The program (which started in 1991 and is ongoing) created a racially integrated "living and learning" community in a 250-student wing of a large dormitory. It focused students on academic work (through weekly "challenge" workshops), provided an outlet for discussing the personal side of college life (through weekly rap sessions), and affirmed the students' abilities (through, for example, reminding them that their admission was a vote of confidence). The program lasted just one semester, although most students remained in the dormitory wing for the rest of their first year.

Still, it worked: it gave Black students a significant academic jump start. Those in the program (about 15 percent of the entering class) got better first-year grades than Black students outside the program, even after controlling for differences between these groups in the skills with which they entered college. Equally important, the program greatly reduced underperformance: Black students in the program got first-year grades almost as high as those of white students in the general Michigan population who entered with comparable test scores. This result signaled the achievement of an academic climate nearly as favorable to Black students as to white students. And it was achieved through a concert of simple things that enabled Black students to feel racially secure.

One tactic that worked surprisingly well was the weekly rap sessions—Black and white students talking to one another in an informal dormitory setting, over pizza, about the personal side of their new lives in college. Participation in these sessions reduced students' feelings of stereotype threat and improved grades. Why? Perhaps when members of one racial group hear members of another racial group express the same concerns they have, the concerns seem less racial. Students may also learn that racial and gender stereotypes are either less at play than they might have feared or don't reflect the worst-feared prejudicial intent. Talking at a personal level across group lines can thus build trust in the larger campus community. The racial segregation besetting most college campuses can block this experience, allowing mistrust to build where cross-group communication would discourage it.

Our research bears a practical message: even though the stereotypes held by the larger society may be difficult to change, it is possible to create niches in which negative stereotypes are not felt to apply. In specific classrooms, within specific programs, even in the climate of entire schools, it is possible to weaken a group's sense of being threatened by negative stereotypes, to allow its members a trust that would otherwise be difficult to sustain. Thus when schools try to decide how important Black-white test-score gaps are in determining the fate of Black students on their campuses and in their schools, they should keep something in mind: for a great portion of Black students the degree of racial trust they feel in their campus life, rather than a few ticks on a standardized test, may be the key to their success.

ASA G. HILLIARD III
(NANA BAFFOUR AMANKWATIA II)

NO MYSTERY: CLOSING THE
ACHIEVEMENT GAP BETWEEN
AFRICANS AND EXCELLENCE

Dr. J. Arthur Jones, Ph.D. in mathematics, formerly employed at the National Academy of Sciences, is one of the great teachers of mathematics in the world. He is particularly successful with low-income African students (I will use "African" instead of "African-American") who are traditionally low performing. He is one of the students of the great teacher/mathematician Dr. Abdulalim Shabazz, who from chairmanships of mathematics at Clark Atlanta University and Lincoln University is responsible directly or indirectly for teaching over half of all the Africans who hold a Ph.D. in mathematics in the United States. Both of these men, and other men and women who were taught by Shabazz, continue to demonstrate that they know how to reach the so-called unteachable. Shabazz once challenged his faculty at Clark Atlanta University in Atlanta, who doubted the intellectual capacities of their students: "Give me your worst ones and I will teach them." His success at doing this is now legendary. About ten years ago, I attended an awards ceremony for outstanding teachers of mathematics at the National Academy of Sciences. Of course, Dr. Shabazz was one of the awardees. Then out of approximately *thirty* awardees, nearly half were former students of Shabazz.

Like Shabazz, Jones has demonstrated time and time again the power of his teaching with low-income African students. Noticeably absent from the language of Shabazz, Jones, and other Shabazz students is the excuse-filled language commonly used to explain the achievement levels of traditionally low-achieving students.

In a book long popular among professionals, *Twice as Less: Black English and the Performance of Black Students in Mathematics and Science,* written by Eleanor Wilson Orr (1987), Orr argues that the performance of African-American students in mathematics and science is crippled by the use of "Black English." Orr's book is merely one of hundreds that purport to explain the typically low performance of African students. In a brief paper titled "Look at Math Teachers, Not Black English," J. Arthur Jones himself demolishes the Orr argument. He challenges both her understanding of "Black Language" and her understanding of and skill in teaching. He points out what she failed to examine, that the quality of instruction is the key element in success or failure.

> As one who has been a mathematician for many years, teaching African-Americans from all socioeconomic groups and at elementary, secondary and university levels throughout the country, I can assure you that Orr's conclusion simply is not true. . . .
>
> Concepts in mathematics and science can be communicated and explained with many tools: the written or spoken work, pictures, diagrams, special symbols, manipulative materials, or a combination of these. If a student fails to understand a mathematical concept, the first place to look for the reason is in the teacher's use of one of these tools of communication. . . .
>
> Moreover, students have a variety of learning styles that influence the difficulty or ease with which they understand certain concepts. Some students learn more easily with some of these communication tools than with others. . . .
>
> Orr's geometry examples reflect a defect in teaching geometry, rather than a defect in the language of the learner. She faults her student, Mary, for not using the linear approach which would have required Mary to place statements and reasons in numbered lines.
>
> However, this method actually may hinder some students as they formulate logical reasons for geometric proofs, because human reasoning generally is not a linear process. It is recursive, connecting what is given to what is to be proved, and it only appears to be linear after a solution has been found. . . .
>
> Orr's African-American students suffered more from a lack of experience with word problems than from their use of "Black English."

Orr fails to acknowledge that the difficulties of many students are shaped by the quality of earlier teaching, materials, teacher expectations, learning experiences, learning styles, interests and motivation. It could be argued that the usage of any particular language has a minor, if any, role in mathematical perception, because concepts can be expressed in any language. . . .

Orr attributes the problem-solving difficulties of African Americans who use the vernacular to poor language skills, but I would attribute such difficulties to poor teaching skills. Poor language usage certainly limits the ability of students to communicate what they know about science and mathematics, and it is a handicap to social advancement. On the other hand, poor teaching is an even greater handicap. Its effects on the individual can be long-lasting, and its consequences for the nation can be disastrous. (Jones 1990, 1–4)

I have quoted at some length from Jones's short paper in order to give some of the flavor of the thinking of this highly successful teacher of mathematics, which differs radically from that of failing teachers. Jones and his mentor, Shabazz, are not the only exemplars of good teaching. I know many other teachers of mathematics who experienced none of the difficulties that Orr argued were typical and crippling, including several I cited in a paper for the National Council of Teachers of Mathematics *Seventy-fifth Anniversary Yearbook:* William Johntz, creator of the Project SEED approach to teaching college-level mathematics to diverse low-income students in elementary school; Professor Everad Barrett, creator of the Professor B. approach known as Contextual Mathematics teaching, who has had outstanding success for years; the Beginning School Mathematics approach for teaching algebra to three-year-olds, using manipulatives, and developed by Louise McKinnon from New Zealand. A whole host of other teachers succeed with their own homegrown approaches to mathematics and other subjects. There are many ways to be successful (Hilliard 1990, 99–114).

I claim some expertise as a former successful mathematics teacher myself. (Successful teaching experience with traditionally low-performing students should be a qualifying criterion for experts who make pronouncements about teaching and learning.) We should not begin with a search for student deficiencies as the explanation for their academic failure or success. Language and cultural diversity, poverty, crime and drug-ridden neighborhoods, single-parent mostly female-headed households may determine opportunity to learn, not capacity to learn. None of the great teachers I know find any use at all for the usual catalogue of excuses, no matter what the academic discipline. The same thing can be said for the great teachers in all of the disciplines.

Therefore, I begin by relying on the foundation of the experience of the teachers who do not fail to produce excellence in academic achievement, regardless of the background of the students. To do so takes us to a radically different place from the premises of the typical conversations, theories, philosophies, and methodologies that are proposed to explain and to improve the achievement of students.

I begin where there is no gap. Or if there is a gap, it is the opposite of the one that people normally find. It is a gap displayed in circumstances where the poor, cultural minorities, Africans often surpass the performances of their more wealthy peers of any ethnic background. Few educators have seen these examples, even though they have always been around and can still be found in virtually all places where large numbers of Africans and others are. In these places, we are free to explore all kinds of pedagogical speculations, since our students are already in the protected environment of the success that good teachers have produced. That is the only place where a worthy dialogue can take place. The very existence of the examples of successful teachers and schools presents a powerful challenge to many of the theories and practices that are supposed to promote student performance or to explain failure.

WHAT DO WE MEAN BY THE GAP?
SOME FALSE GAPS FIRST

Before exploring in detail the promise that excellent teachers and excellent schools represent, let me say explicitly what I think about "gaps" commonly touted in educational research. There is an important gap, but it is not the one most writers come close to addressing. First, some false gaps.

In the past, there have really been two purported gaps that have captured the attention of educators and the general public. On the one hand, there is the so-called achievement gap, which I examine below. Then there is the supposed gap in "intelligence" between Africans and Europeans. This second theorized gap is popular enough still among certain researchers to merit examining.

The perennial "fifteen-point gap," or "the one-standard-devia-tion gap" in statistical terms, between the mean score of Africans and the mean score of Europeans on "intelligence tests," or "IQ tests," is the source of the belief in an intelligence gap. Of course, adherents assume that standardized IQ tests are valid measures of human capacity. And indeed, many authors have concluded that the current low performance of African students on IQ tests is, in fact, normal, and that a gap in achievement can be expected, because they believe that there is a genetically based incapacity of African students to match European students' test performance.

Two widely read texts, which together represent volumes of similar literature, are Arthur Jensen's *Bias in Mental Tests* (1980) and Richard Herrnstein and Charles Murray' s *The Bell Curve* (1994). To blunt any protest that these texts represent bizarre opinions, I note that empirical study of the opinions of elite researchers and scholars reveal that, in general, they agree with the Jensen, Herrnstein, and Murray findings on mental measurement. They believe that IQ tests are valid measures of mental capacity. That is, these experts believe that there is a real gap in intelligence between Africans and Europeans, rather than a gap in opportunity. These opinions are documented in a survey study by Mark Snyderman and Stanley Rothman (1988).

Since this is not an essay about testing and its results, and in particular not a critique of the mental measurement movement, I will refer merely to the critical bibliography documenting the absence of validity evidence for IQ tests (Rowe 1991; Hilliard 1994, 1995; Houts 1977; Gould 1981; Kamin 1974; Donovan and Cross 2002). Present science, technology, and mental measurement are fundamentally incapable of measuring human capacity. Therefore Black and white differences in that capacity cannot be measured. Intelligence tests are nothing more than a particular kind of "achievement test" that favors students who have a privileged opportunity to be exposed to those things being measured on the tests. Yes, there is a perennial gap in scores on tests that purport to measure native intelligence. The question is what the scores mean. The scores represent "achievement," not intelligence. No instruments exist at this time to perform a valid measure to document an intelligence gap between and among any human groups, or even within a given group.

I might add at the same that there is no construct validity for "intelligence." At a recent global meeting of elite psychologists in Melbourne, Australia, held to consider the meaning of intelligence and its valid measure, one of the most significant outcomes was the admission that there was no consensus among the experts on the meaning of intelligence. Hence, there can be no possibility of its measurement in a way that allows questions about it to be treated scientifically (Rowe 1991). At least one major respected scientific institution, the National Research Council of the National Academy of Sciences, has recently issued its report on disproportion in special education (Donovan and Cross 2002). This was the second report on the same topic in twenty years. The committee concluded that IQ tests are worthless for making decisions about student placement in programs for those who are mentally retarded, gifted, or learning disabled. This conclusion is enormously important. It is a stunning setback for those professionals who advocate IQ, if they are awake to scientific data. A few of the findings that follow literally strike at the heart of current special education theory and practice:

> No contemporary test author or publisher endorses the notion that IQ tests are direct measures of innate ability. Yet misconceptions that the tests reflect genetically determined, innate ability that is fixed throughout the life span remain prominent with the public, many educators, and some social scientists. Moreover, test authors and test publishers all acknowledge that IQ tests are measures of what individuals have learned —that is, it is useful to think of them as tests of general achievement, reflecting broad, culturally rooted ways of thinking and solving problems. The tests are only indirect measures of success with the school curriculum and imperfect predictors of school achievement.

And so, I leave the intelligence gap discussion with this statement: "There is no there there." The current use of intelligence testing in education is a meaningless practice that offers us no help in understanding the differences in achievement between Africans and others.

Arguments for the tests' use should rest in peace, though I doubt that they will. They will probably persist for reasons that have nothing to do with science and pedagogy.

But there is another "gap" in education debates. It has become popular to refer to one of the perennial problems in education, that of low achievement by the large majority of African students, as "the achievement gap," that is, the gap between the average performance of African students and the average performance of European students.

Note that when speaking of "the achievement gap" it is understood by virtually everyone that this does not refer to a gap between Africans and Asians or a gap between Africans and Latinos or a gap between Africans and anyone else other than Europeans. Therefore, right away, it seems that something more than achievement is being discussed when the gap language is used.

Framing the problem in this way is itself problematic. Importantly, it establishes European average achievement as the universal norm, no matter what the quality of achievement may be, even if it is mediocre. Certainly dialogue about the gap is seldom followed up by a detailed analysis of the achievements of the norm group. Closer scrutiny is usually heaped on those who perform poorly than on those who "succeed." Reexamining the norm group's achievement would reveal that the typical discussion about "the norm" really may be a discussion about normative mediocrity.

In almost all comparative international studies of achievement, among nations within the "developed world," the United States ranks near last. Only if comparisons are made between a small percentage of elite students, who have been given extraordinary opportunities, do we find that there is some parity among the global elites, so that the United States holds its own. In a way, therefore, we may suspect that prolonged dialogue about "the gap," and analysis of low performers, may actually contribute to a continuation of relatively mediocre results in general, and to a continued depression of the achievement of African students in particular. This is because many Americans take comfort in performances that are "excellent" only in relationship to perennial low performance. All children deserve much better than this in terms of educator expectations. I believe that this narrowness of focus is the legacy of slavery, segregation, and the ideology of white supremacy and in large measure allows us to be satisfied with mediocrity, even for the elite. Oppression drags everyone down. The legacy of oppression has not been overcome. Equal opportunity to learn does not yet exist (Kozol 1991; Donovan and Cross 2002; Delpit 1995).

Excellence should be judged based upon criterion levels of performance, not relative levels. This gets us away from the "Black White achievement gap." For example, years ago the College Board (1983) published a "Green Book" on what students should know and be able to do at graduation from high school. This book articulated what were essentially college preparatory standards. The standards were developed by a multidisciplinary and multiethnic group. In my opinion, these standards were rigorous and fair. Although there can always be improvement in the standards, these are the types of objectives that help educators to aim for high criterion levels of performance. The gap between the present level of performance for African students and the criterion performance standards that should be required is the academic achievement gap that must be closed. Too often, by using the European students' normative performance as the universal standard, not only do we use a low standard, but we tend to be satisfied with the performance of minority cultural groups when a substantial reduction in this gap occurs. The unconscious assumption seems to be that the traditional low performers cannot surpass—merely approach— the performance of the norm group.

THE GAP BETWEEN AFRICAN ACHIEVEMENT AND EXCELLENCE

There can be no question but that the achievement of African students is, in general, far below their potential. This gap, however, should not be thought of as the gap between Black and white students. It should be thought of as the gap between the current performance of African students and levels of excellence. When we choose excellent performance as the goal, academically and socially, we change the teaching and learning paradigm in fundamental ways. By setting the required performance level at excellence, we require excellent performance to be articulated.

Although there will not be universal agreement on what constitutes excellence in particular cases, it is, in my experience, possible to develop operational definitions and some consensus that will take us far along the road we need to travel. For example, there are clear cases. As a former mathematics teacher, I find that, usually without much debate, many educators are able to agree that the accomplishments of Project SEED and of the Marcus Garvey School in Los Angeles represent excellent achievement. In those programs, teachers are able to teach higher mathematics to traditionally low-performing student groups, at ages earlier than more privileged groups normally are introduced to the subject. Specifically, Marcus Garvey offers a course in calculus at the fifth grade, something many of us believe is high-level achievement in content, in difficulty, and in complexity, to students for whom many had predicted even low-level arithmetic to be beyond their means. It can be done anywhere. As we will see, there is no magic, just good teaching.

Some years ago, Dr. Barbara Sizemore and I coedited a report of the Taskforce for Black Academic and Cultural Excellence for the National Alliance of Black Educators (Hilliard and Sizemore 1984). In it we identified performance standards at criterion levels for various subject areas. We argued for criteria levels of performance at high school graduation that looked a great deal like college preparatory work currently proposed in general. In other words, we believed then and now that current college preparatory course work is well within the reach of the general population, including the population of African students currently performing "below the norm," even within the first quartile.

Our thinking on the criterion levels of performance is in essential harmony with two of the recent education reports, the College Board's *Academic Preparation for College: What Students Need to Know and Be Able to Do,* and the *Paidea Proposal* by Mortimer Adler (1982). These are not unreasonable goals for African-American students, if fair, equitable, appropriate, and high-quality instructional support is offered to them (Hilliard and Sizemore 1984, 35–36).

So there is an achievement gap. To me the gap between Africans and Europeans is a nonissue. The real gap is between Africans' typical performance and the criterion levels of excellence, which are well within the reach of the masses of them. That is the gap that is unacceptable, given what we know about what good teaching can do, and given what we know about the genius of our children (Wilson 1990).

THE OPPORTUNITY TO LEARN GAP:
THE QUALITY OF SERVICE

There is another gap, one that is rarely acknowledged. It is a gap that has been submerged in the dialogue about intelligence and achievement because of a paradigm of human incapacity, especially pessimistic with respect to African students. This gap is the quality-of-service gap. No one has described it better than Jonathon Kozol (1991). It is the gap that he refers to as "savage inequalities." Nothing is more peculiar than the continuing seeming inability of our leading educators to acknowledge these well-documented savage inequalities and to use them as the basis for explaining the academic, social, and cultural achievements of students.

In my early studies in science classes, I was introduced to the idea of the "law of parsimony," which simply states that when choosing the most probable explanations for certain research results, it is often best to accept the simplest explanation in preference to more complicated alternatives. This is because, on balance, the simplest explanations tend to be more valid in the long run. That is certainly true in the case of education. Nonetheless convoluted explanations for differential achievement abound, recently cast in terms of neuroscience and psychology, having to do with the number of intelligences in the brain, or whether it's the left side or the right side that is working, or whether there is enough "hard disk space" in the student's brain. or whether there is a "fast enough processor." All take the focus of professional attention away from quality control of services provided, and all tend to ignore the matter of opportunity to learn.

A review of research from the past century will reveal that the overwhelming body of inquiry has been focused on child deficiencies. Only a minuscule number of references have focused on "savage inequalities" in service. And yet when inequalities are studied, we have seen some of the most productive research in education. Efforts such as those by Shirley Brythe Heath (1983), Lisa Delpit (1995), and others have looked far beyond before-and-after instruction comparisons of student achievement gains to ask for clarity on the process of education as well. Their work has been very fruitful in illuminating what would otherwise be obscure. (Unfortunately, research requires that meaningful sources of variation be controlled for in studies of teaching and learning. These requirements are seldom met.)

David Berliner and Bruce Biddle (1996) have suggested that at least some critics of public education choose to emphasize the diversionary work of public school bashing in order to avoid the more appropriate work of honest documentation of school effects. They charge myth and fraud in some of the prominent research on public education and its effects. In other words, Berliner and Biddle challenge the will of many critics of public education to provide equality and opportunity to learn for all children. They suggest that some critics of public education obscure the work of public education in order to divert attention from the larger matters of income inequality and inequality and inadequacy in the provision of resources for schools.

It is my belief that behind this is a common, widely shared ideology, driven by a Bell Curve paradigm, with its origin in slavery, colonization, the ideology of white supremacy, and the legacy of segregation and apartheid. I take very little time here to document these matters, which are well attested in the literature (Guthrie 1998; Weinberg 1977). The history of white supremacy ideology and behavior in its current form, "racism," is well covered in the literature (Hilliard 2001; Gossett 1973; etc.). The blend of that ideology and behavior with psychological and educational practice is also extremely well documented (Kamin 1974; Gould 1981; Guthrie 1998). In other words, there is a belief system and a behavior system in education, and in the supporting academic disciplines, that provide the rationale for the continuation of brutal pessimism with respect to African students, and for inappropriate pedagogical responses to the African condition. Not only do these ideological positions exist, but the more important problem is that, in general, educators are in denial about their existence. Hence the need for explicit documentation of the savage inequalities, and the need for staff development and education of educators and the public in general about the savage inequalities. Otherwise, the error and propaganda about the absence of capacity of African students and the failure to provide the appropriate resources will persist.

GAP CLOSERS NOW AND THEN, HERE AND THERE: TEACHER, SCHOOL, AND WHOLE DISTRICTS

There is no mystery. There has never been a time in American education when there have not been "gap closers," that is, teachers and school leaders who demonstrate their capability to move students who typically perform in the lower quartile by standardized tests measures even into the top quartile, indeed in some cases into the lead position within their schools and districts.

I have lived with and among excellent teachers all of my life. My mother, father, two aunts, an uncle, and numerous other relatives and friends were teachers in the segregated schools of Texas. I have seen great teaching and outstanding schools, not only among my family and friends, but also among thousands of teachers and schools worldwide. You may use any criteria for good schools that you chose: standardized test scores, course completion in rigorous subjects, character development, socialization, spiritual development, excellence in performing arts, independent avid reading, leadership, and so on. There are educators, working in even the most difficult circumstances, who rarely fail to get excellent outcomes, far beyond "closing the gap" and grade level performance.

These teachers and schools were not preoccupied wondering about their students' intelligence. Successful educators, producers of excellence, whom I knew and observed, worried a lot about their students' opportunities to learn, and about their own teaching, not about students' intelligence.

To a large extent these teachers who produce excellence are unknown and all but invisible. Yet the very success of my Texas teachers, and my good teachers later in the integrated schools in Colorado, represented a fundamental challenge to the conventional wisdom in teacher education and educational research, theory, and practice. These teachers worked, applying old methods, in old school structures, without Ritalin, without vouchers, with rudimentary theoretical notions, with low technologies, and with no standardized cookie-cutter "research-based" programs or centralized micromanagement of the instructional process. For them, IQ scores did not predict school achievement, cultural deprivation theory did not explain school achievement, sociological theories about the correlation of socioeconomic status with student measured "capacity" and achievement were irrelevant.

On the other hand, the professional literature was, and still is, filled with student, family, and cultural deficit theories, proposed minimum competency remedies, reflecting a terrible pessimism about the power of teachers, schools, and children.

It is a peculiarity of how research questions are framed in education that obscures these examples from the view of researchers. Some researchers prefer large sample sizes, controlled experiments, large minimum-competency, cookie-cutter programs, preferring to ignore single instances of atypical high performance with poor children as "outliers" or errors. Even long-running large-scale successful programs such as William Johntz's Project SEED, which we will examine, and Stanley Pogrow's HOTS (Higher Order Thinking Skills) are often overlooked. Although more typical programs and practices are certainly interesting and worthy of research interest, from my experience the more fruitful question to ask is, Where are the examples of highest achievements with typically low-performing students? And then, in the first phase at least, if that's a single class, a single school, or a single school district, closer examination is justified, probably with ethnographic methodologies, in order to understand the processes that account for such radical departure from predicted performance. The typical and more favored work of educational researchers of having large sample sizes and the like can then be considered a second phase in research to validate or verify the principles involved when powerful teachers and powerful schools are in operation.

Happily, we now have sufficient evidence from a variety of sources to demonstrate just how easy it is to produce high achievement in typically low-performing schools. While such achievement could have been found in the past, contemporary efforts have been documented in such works as Schmoker 1999; Haycock 1999; Sizemore 1988; Sizemore, Brosard, and Harrigan 1994; Saunders and Rivers 1996; Comer 1980; Hughes 1995; Jones 1981; Ladson-Billings 1994; Levine and Lezotte 1990; Watson and Smitherman 1996; and others. These studies document excellence, not adequacy.

Typically, in communities where children have a history of low performance, educators have tended to be satisfied with "grade level" performance, even below-grade-level performance. That is because those educators have an implicit Bell Curve ideology in mind. Projects such as the Edison Project and Success for All are then able to sell themselves to school districts by claiming victory, when "the experimental group scores five percentile ranks higher than the control group." A trivial difference in achievement between two sets of schools in the lower quartile or lower half of the achievement distribution is seen as great, when neither experimental nor control is at or above grade level in performance. No elite private school would accept such services, which may be why they are marketed to poor people, usually minorities in large urban districts.

Evaluation research shows that extraordinarily high achievement gains can be made, in a relatively brief period, by relatively simple approaches, in spite of typical challenges, for the lowest-income students, regardless of race. For example, there are few educational research results more stunning than that of William Saunders and J. C. Rivers (1996). They were able to show that by providing three good teachers in a row to students as they took third, fourth, and fifth grade mathematics, and comparing them with students who had three weaker teachers in a row, the students with the good teachers showed achievement fifty percentile ranks higher than those whose opportunities to learn were obviously impeded by poor teaching! Few studies in the history of education provide more support for teaching effects than this one. These results present a fundamental challenge to IQ ideology, to methodologies for evaluating school effects, and to the "brutal pessimism" about human capacity. Many other examples confirm such teaching effects.

So let's put the capacity issue to bed; let's put the fact that so many educators are puzzled on the table. Let's not ask them for advice or leadership. Let's take African students whose learning potential is enormous and move them up where they belong.

A recent *New York Times* story charted the rise over the past few years of a new group of dominant schools in the world of competitive high school "Mock Trials" (McDougall 1999). In this intellectual sport, traditionally dominated by elite schools, where participants take the roles of attorneys in arguing cases based in real law, "schools with poor academic achievement have consistently risen through the championship ranks." In New York and Philadelphia a tradition of high achievement in this high-pressure arena has emerged:

- "Philadelphia's inner-city schools have finished first or second in the last three Pennsylvania championships, beating elite suburban schools."
- "Overbrook High School [in Philadelphia] jumped from its spot on the city's academic-warning list into the No. 1 spot on the state's Mock Trial teams . . . finishing 11th in the nation. . . . Every member of the team was a rookie, recruited and trained by a history teacher who also doubled as a baseball coach."
- "Carver High School, from North Philadelphia's notorious Badlands, won the city championship and defeated dozens of prep and private schools to finish second in the state finals."
- "In Manhattan, the team to beat is Louis D. Brandeis High School, which has nearly as many dropouts as graduates."

John C. Shipley, coach of a national championship and Mock Trial handbook author, summarizes the trend: "The inner-city kids have been putting on a regular magic show the last couple of years. Schools you never heard of in the past, except for maybe gang problems or poor academics, are suddenly taking the competitions by storm."

The transformation of individual students and the creation of new thriving cultures of achievement in schools have impressed observers—and surprised them (although it should not have, I would argue). The reporter writes, "What's most surprising is the kind of students being drawn to the activity." And then, quoting an observer: "If you go by the statistics, these are the kinds of kids who should be having trouble with the law, not enjoying it." The performance of Carver High School's Davyses McLaurin, a "former class clown" voted Pennsylvania's "top litigator," left people's mouths "literally agape at what he was coming up with," according to David Trevaskis of Temple University Law School's high school outreach program.

Expert observers note that the pace and culture of national Mock Trials have changed, as the new champions make their distinctive mark and presumably inspire each other to new levels of performance. The nature of the courtroom arguments has changed—more "hotly contested," with "rapid-fire objections." And the new style has raised levels of performance across the board. Deborah Lesser, coordinator of the New York City Mock Trials, says that "students are sharper, more nimble on their feet, more in command of rules and strategy and presentation." She continues: "There's no comparison between then and now." John Shipley adds: "Nowadays, if you lose focus for a minute, you lose."

What happened at Brooklyn's Bushwick High School, Manhattan's Brandies High School, and Philadelphia's Overbrook High School and Carver High School? What IQ or achievement test score, previous grade point average, student behavior, family background, socioeconomic status, or parent marital status would have predicted that the individual student moot court winners would have moved from one end of the bell curve to the other in achievement?

This intellectual achievement is certainly as high as it gets. Not only do the students of traditionally low-performing ethnic groups and income levels do well, but they excel, defeating even the wealthy suburban elites, soundly. Moreover, they changed the game, picking up the pace, bringing a more aggressive cultural style, performing even more complicated and more intellectual feats than ever before, in the memory of the sponsors and coaches.

My son Hakim Hilliard had an almost identical experience with a street law class that he taught at Georgetown University Law School when he was a student there. The students in his class from the inner city put on a stellar performance in their moot court appearance before faculty and students at Georgetown Law School. They grasped fine nuances of law. They were aggressive. They were fast. They were confident, almost arrogant. The transformation can be virtually instantaneous. Students who were holding back not only accept tough academic challenges, but thrive on them. Further, they even bring new power to the game. I know of many other equally dramatic examples of excellence from African, First Nations students and poor children.

The only major change in the lives of the students above is that they were exposed to good teaching. It is just that simple. It happens all the time.

And yet why do we act as if these magnificent transformations did not occur? Will we say that we have to wait until students change their attitudes, fears, and perceptions on their own before they can be taught? Will we call for therapy and counseling to resolve their problems of low academic self-esteem? The great teachers do not see it that way at all.

Popular explanations for low performance of African students help to frame approaches to service that will ultimately limit the capacities of students. Once such explanation is the "acting white" explanation. A few African researchers, along with others, have become enamored with this explanation. They argue in their research that African students fail because they think that achievement means that they would "become white." Some researchers find that many African students are opposed to being successful in school subjects because of peer pressure. Some students are said to be opposed to the school curriculum. Some researchers have such simple explanations, which are widely accepted I might add, probably because the explanations fit the preferred paradigm of many educational consumers.

I do not doubt that students tell researchers that they think to achieve at a high level is to "act white." I do not doubt that students value their peers and do not want to loose peer approval. The problem is, do these orientations appear under all conditions, especially under the conditions of inspired teaching? There is something sterile and antiseptic about the finely executed, dispassionate, and trivial studies of low-performing students. "On the ground," things are often very different. I would call children's disaffected responses to researchers "sour grapes" responses. Their "opposition" seems always to disappear when the means to save these students—good teaching—is provided. But whatever students may say, it must be considered against a backdrop of similar students whose lives have been transformed by inspired high-quality education. As the above example suggests, even if students respond to researchers in the ways described above, they still are candidates for academic excellence. They have genius that must be tapped.

Many of the same students, supposedly debilitated by their avoidance of "acting white," damaged by "rumors of inferiority," or avoiding intellectual work because of peer pressure, have been turned around virtually in an instant to dominate chess tournaments, to become fierce competitors in street law programs, to become writers, mathematicians, and the like.

The experience of gap closers is significantly different from the popular professional explanations for failure. A recent National Academy of Sciences National Research Council report includes a section that debunks this myth about the opposition of inner-city children to excellence in academic achievement.

Similarly, Jeffrey Howard and Ray Hammond in "Rumors of Inferiority" (1985) suggest that African students do not achieve because they accept and internalize the rumors of their inferiority among those who serve them. Again, as with the "acting white" hypothesis, it may well be that some students internalize these things. However, gap closers have a very different experience with these same students.

Socioeconomic status and crime are another set of factors that are used to explain low performance among African students. Once again, this must be submitted to the gap closers test. Do gap closers find socioeconomic status and crime to be effects so debilitating that students are barred from achieving excellence and closing the gap between their current performance and the excellent level? The answer is no!

And finally, there is the "critical periods" explanation coming from studies on imprinting in birds and other psychological data. This theory seems to be widely held among educators. It is this: if certain types of achievement do not occur at an early age, then the capacities that underlie those achievements will be diminished. It is thought that it will then be impossible for students to close the gap between what they could have done and what they now are able to do. Once more, we must ask the question, Do gap closers find this to be the case? The roll call of gap closers reveals that almost to the person, they say exactly the opposite. Abdulalim Shabazz, Sinichi Suzuki (1984), this author (Hilliard 1991), and many others have demonstrated that this is simply a false hypothesis. It can persist only because there is a desire to have it persist among some people, or because of ignorance. There is absolutely no excuse for this ignorance, and certainly no excuse for the false and invalid continued use of these hypotheses.

CLASSROOMS AND TEACHERS

What makes gap-closing success possible? What features do such successful programs and teaching share? What do they look and feel like?

Consider these other paradigmatic stories of gap closers—at the program, individual, and whole school level. These stories should be our starting point for understanding African school achievement.

More than thirty years ago, I was living in Liberia, West Africa. An article appeared in either *Time* or *Newsweek* that caught my eye. The article reported on a demonstration conducted by William Johntz, a teacher at Berkeley High School in California, where elementary school children in fifth and sixth grade were learning college-level algebra material. I had long since become jaded and suspicious in my expectations of education programs that claimed to produce high achievement with low-income, cultural minority children. Too many such programs had turned out to produce little real achievement, and sometimes they had actually produced less achievement than was normal. There have been many hustlers in public education who have found a way to profit from public education without providing significant benefits for students. I soon discovered that Project SEED, Bill Johntz's program, was not one of these.

When my assignment in Liberia came to an end in 1970, the first person I contacted upon my return was William Johntz. I wanted to see what he was doing. I wanted to verify the results that were being reported. Bill Johntz told me that he would talk to me about the project only if I would attend a demonstration with the children. I was excited, to say the least.

My son and I attended a demonstration for the San Francisco Public School System's teachers. A regular sixth grade class, all African, from a poor neighborhood, was on the stage. They were in their fifth day of instruction. Using only a piece of chalk and a blackboard, William Johntz took the students through their paces. He gave a brief explanation about who the students were, and a few minimal things about Project SEED, for about five minutes. Then he began to teach.

The class came alive! The lesson was about logarithms and exponentiation. The whole method involved the use of Socratic questioning. Johntz told the students very little, rather required the students to solve the problems as a consequence of questioning. The questioning was used to probe the student's understanding of concepts and operations, to probe to discover the assumptions that the students were using, in order to respond to questions. Then questions were used to determine where the whole class stood on the responding student's answer. Hand signals revealed instantly whether students agreed or disagreed with a response. Then Johntz would sample those who agreed or disagreed. Sometimes he would take a student who gave an unexpected answer to a question, then after probing to discover the student's assumptions and definitions, use that student's logic and follow up with more questions that assumed the logic of that student, to see where it would lead. More questions were then asked to determine agreement or disagreement. Students were encouraged to use their "gestures of intellectual protest," a hand signal where hands were waved in front of and across the body. The idea here was to build students' confidence and willingness to take a position, even if it was not the popular one. By treating every answer as worthy of examination, most students did indeed take positions, challenge them, and listen carefully to others.

In this type of classroom, it was very difficult for a student to be inactive or not to be engaged. Many techniques were used to generate meaningful moment-to-moment participation. Students were asked to choose other students for responses. The teacher alternated in questioning students who agreed and those who disagreed. The teacher showed much more interest in discovering the reasoning of students than in the "right" answer. Students were learning obviously high-level content and were highly motivated by their ability to do so. Care was taken to call on every student. This was whole class instruction, not catering to a small group. The teacher was constantly on the move, checking written work at each desk, making comments about the written work to the students, calling students' names out loud with some specific comment about the student's work that reflected good thinking. The teacher was more like a conductor than a lecturer. The energy in the classroom was enormous. The students seemed to enjoy the audience of one hundred or so teachers and the responses that they gave to the students' performances.

It was quite clear from the outset that to be free to function in this way the teacher would have to have deep knowledge in mathematics, something that is very rare among public school teachers. There is no way that the line of questions in response to students' responses could be framed in an instant if the teacher did not know his or her subject in depth. Many teachers teach outside their fields or receive most of their preparation in methodology rather than in content. It was also clear, in the relaxed classroom atmosphere, even though all students were intensively engaged in thinking, that the relationships between students and the teacher and among students were very socially supportive and reinforcing.

To take students who perform typically two to three years below grade level in arithmetic and engage them in high-level conceptually oriented mathematics within a few days is a wonderful sight to see. It challenges a whole host of common assumptions among educators about teaching and learning—assumptions about methodology, student mental capacity, student mental health and behavioral characteristics, and so on.

Many evaluation studies have been performed on Project SEED. Even though the students in the program are being taught algebra, trigonometry, and even calculus more recently, they gain about two years in arithmetic scores on standardized achievement for each single year of instruction. This means significant gains in *arithmetic achievement* and *mathematics achievement,* enormous gains in *academic self-concept and self-esteem,* and improvement in *communication and social skills.*

It is very difficult for discipline problems to emerge in Project SEED classes, since virtually all students are fully engaged in time on task. I have seen the students listening carefully to their peers, since they very likely will be called upon to respond to their peers. Observers can feel the excitement. When I worked in Portland, Oregon, as a consultant to the school district, I arranged for the area assistant superintendents for instruction to visit Project SEED in Dallas for nearly two weeks. During their visit, they were able to visit several SEED classes at random. Upon their return, I asked if any of the three assistant superintendents had observed any discipline problems in any class. The answer in each case was no.

Here is an approach that has worked magnificently. It has only grown more powerful with age. Hundreds of teachers have been trained to teach according to the Project SEED approach. And yet I have learned over the years that Project SEED remains relatively unknown among mathematics teacher educators, mathematics teachers, mathematics staff developers, and among educators and the general public as well. How can this be? Is it that they know of a better alternative, better in terms of achievement outcomes?

A TEACHER: CARRIE SECRET

Carrie Secret is known to many now as one of the teachers who was at the center of the Ebonics controversy in the Oakland Unified School District in California, beginning in December 1996. She has been a teacher at the Prescott School in West Oakland, a high-poverty and virtually all African school. It is a school where normal expectations were that the children would not succeed, academically or socially. It is a school where it was expected that parents, mostly single mothers, do not care. It is a school where large numbers of the children were expected to be relegated to special education. It is the school that Carrie Secret calls home.

Carrie Secret describes herself as "*ten* years old," referring to her cultural rebirth as an African. This rebirth is every bit as important for her as for her students, for both personal and pedagogical reasons. She loves children, learning, and her people. Carrie Secret has always had a personal commitment to her students, seldom matched by that of other teachers. For example, she refused to leave her first graders at the end of their year with her, staying with them and their families as their teacher until the students completed their work at Prescott. Carrie has always seen herself as a member of the families of all of her students. She demonstrates that she is willing to do whatever it takes to ensure their survival and their success.

Carrie Secret often takes her students to professional meetings to demonstrate their achievements, and their brilliance in general. In public performances, the children showcase their phenomenal memories, as they present spirited interpretive renderings of great African literature, the poetry of Ilyana Vansant, the sermons of the great Reverend Jeremiah Wright, the thirty-four-hundred-year-old Egyptian wisdom teachings of Ptahhotep, creative essays researched and written by Secret, among many other writings. The short public presentations cannot capture the essence of the hours of study that the teacher and students must do in preparation. Students are not permitted merely to do rote presentations.

To visit Carrie Secret's class is to enter a truly intellectual world, and a very spiritual one as well. The walls are covered with charts, art, and short selections of masterpieces of literature. The faces are predominantly Africans; however, a child of any ethnic background is honored by having the whole class learn about his or her cultural background. These materials are incorporated seamlessly into the regular classroom work in all disciplines.

Of course this means that Carrie Secret must be a scholar in the truest sense of that word. I have conversed with her for several years about her reading interests and about her mission and purpose for pursuing them. She chooses difficult scholarly work, selecting those that document the truth about African people and their culture. She also includes materials that confront racism and white supremacy behavior head on.

Secret's children engage in the classroom in critical analysis and commentary on these matters. In other words, the readings and other materials are brought to the children, with teacher mediation to help the children have access to the readings and materials. Carrie Secret could have children reading Dr. Seuss, Donald Duck, Harry Potter, or any of the typical reading or "enrichment" materials that many children get. However, Carrie Secret never talks down to her children, even the youngest ones. She thinks that even the most difficult and challenging ideas are accessible, in large measure, to all of the children.

Secret's classes are full of movement and action, much of it collective. The children sing and dance to serious themes. They do art and write stories and essays. They play games. All of these things are for a purpose.

Each child is regarded as a spiritual being. That spirit can be crushed or lifted up by one of the most important people in the life of that child, his or her teacher. No conversation with Secret about her children can go on long before you see that she knows each child name by name. She knows special things about them, their personal and family crises. She knows how they are progressing in other classes in the school, even maintaining contact with graduates from Prescott. Carrie Secret is their advocate as well as teacher.

Many of Carrie Secret's children were labeled as needing special education. Of course, Secret ignored the classifications, and the children did too. She treated them as scholars, and they behaved that way.

Recently, I reviewed a video program that was made shortly after the "Ebonics Controversy" in Oakland. It featured Carrie Secret's class of fifth graders. It took more than an hour to videotape the interview, which was done live in Secret's classroom, while the children continued their work in the background. During the entire time, the students worked together in small groups on various academic projects. There was no disorder, no fighting. Occasionally the video showed Carrie Secret as she detected the noise level rise to an unacceptable level somewhere in the classroom. In the African way, Secret would simply say, "Ago?" This is a request for students' attention and a reminder of the requirements for work. The whole class was then required to respond, "Amee!" This meant, you have our attention and we agree to work as required. At no point during the interview, as shown on the raw footage of the tape, did children get out of order. As the camera panned the room, they engaged eagerly in their work in their small groups.

Secret's students identify strongly with her. The relationship is more motherly than manager, more scientist than preacher or lecturer, more coach and partner in investigations than passive supervisor of a sterile commercial program.

Parents and community are vital to Carrie Secret. They attend the frequent programs in which their children perform, often traveling to demonstrations when time allows. They are often the proud observers at events when the press or visitors come to Prescott. Secret is in their homes. She makes demands of them for assistance. She confers with them about student problems and successes. The bond is strong and clear.

If someone goes to Prescott Elementary School to try to discover the "method" or "technique" that Carrie Secret uses to transform these students into academic high achievers, they will probably find little that is novel. The uniqueness is in the quality of the implementation of good instructional practices. Respecting prior knowledge, valuing and creating human bonds, studying for deep knowledge, respecting students, respecting parents, respecting communities are all accepted by many professionals, at a verbal level. The actuality in most classrooms leaves much to be desired.

However, we can say something about Secret's distinctive process. Her success seems to be a product precisely of her deep continuing study to expand her knowledge of her subjects, African history and culture, and the study of racism and its manifestations; her close family relationship with her students and their families and community: her uncompromising commitment to get her students to achieve at the excellence level, by any means necessary; her linkage to a network of teachers who share her sense of commitment and mission; her willingness, her keen sense of social justice, and her sense of duty to save the children and to save African people, and others, from the negative fate that awaits many of them.

Carrie Secret's work is a powerful example that typical professional concern with a limited set of parameters, for example, methods and techniques, although important in some ways, is far from the most important part of the matter. Are students and their families and communities loved and respected to the extent that their teachers and school leaders will take nothing less than excellent outcomes, academically, socially, physically, and spiritually?

Teachers like Carrie Secret, projects like Project SEED, and even whole successful schools like Sankofa Schule in East Lansing, Michigan, or Chick Elementary School in Kansas City, Missouri, are frequent targets of school leaders. The are seen often as "not team players." They do not fit the programs that are "research based." They are almost always ignored in typical research studies. As a result, we have lost many opportunities to inspire other professionals, to inform policy makers, to challenge bad educational psychology, bad educational sociology, and bad pedagogy. The feeling seems to be that these teachers are unique or charismatic, and that what they do is beyond other teachers. Nothing could be further from the truth. These examples lead where we should go.

We will never solve the problem of how to raise the level of African children to excellence as long as we restrict our vision to management, organizational structures, text materials, and other efficiency-driven models. We must create the professional environments to nurture people like William Johntz and his associates and Carrie Secret.

WHOLE SCHOOL: FROM FAILURE
TO EXCELLENCE IN ONE YEAR

Over the years I've seen many schools transformed. Some have even moved from worst to first within a very short period of time. Although there are a few evaluations, ethnographies, and videotape or film summaries of schools that change, the actual patterns or structure for change are not apparent. Highly successful schools, like Harmony-Leland Elementary School, in Cobb County, Georgia, rarely come to the attention of educators.

About four years ago, I was given the opportunity by Cobb County superintendent Benjamin to present some of my videotaped examples of outstanding schools that serve urban poor children. These videotapes were presented at a countywide staff development workshop. I like to show ten to fifteen examples of stunning "turn-around cases," both for the effect that they have on participants, most of whom have never seen even one such example, and in order to show the diverse approaches taken to reach the common goal of excellent academic student achievement.

I choose deliberately to show schools in the poorest sections of their cities, because the forecast for student achievement tends to be uniformly low. This demonstrates that many educators have no problem teaching poor African children. I also choose examples of excellence, rather than grade-level, as the criterion level of performance for the students. This is an attempt to totally do away with the specious arguments that blame impediments—for example, poverty and single-parent families—for making high achievement "impossible" for poor children. I like to show schools that are "racially integrated" as well as "racially isolated," where children in either case have achieved excellence. I like to show bilingual as well as monolingual services for children of Latino background, or other backgrounds, to show that excellence is possible under both conditions. In short, I attempt to show that there really is no mystery about how to teach children class by class, school by school, or district by district, for some educators.

Sandra McGary was in the audience at one of my staff development presentations. At the time, she was one of the chief assistants to the superintendent of the Cobb County Public Schools. She showed great interest in that workshop, and especially in the videotaped examples of successful schools. She arranged for me to come back to the Cobb County Schools to speak with other educational leaders. Shortly after those meetings, Sandra McGary decided to approach the superintendent to request an opportunity to lead a school herself, saying that she had become convinced by what she saw that she could do what others had done.

McGary was assigned to one of the lowest-performing schools in Cobb County in the fall of 1999. Within a single year, the school became one of the higher-performing schools in Cobb County.

In the fall of 2000, a special school opening included an auditorium filled with family and community, with three featured guests. One of them was the secretary of education, Richard Riley. Another was the head of the Grammy Awards, who presented an award and some resources to Harmony-Leland School. The third guest was the son of Leonard Bernstein, who also presented an award to the school for achievement. One of the curriculum foci at Harmony-Leland School is performing arts. However, their achievement was high in language arts and mathematics, as well as in performing arts. In other words, there was across-the-board achievement.

The spirit at Harmony-Leland was and is high, so high that every visitor picks it up. I have had occasion to send many observers to Harmony-Leland, sometimes several faculty members from a single school, sometimes students from my courses in social and cultural foundations of education or psychology of the inner-city child. This was just so that they could know that, within a fifteen-minute drive for most of them, is one of the most outstanding schools in the state of Georgia, indeed in the nation. "Ms. McBeautiful" as Sandra McGary is known to her students, is everywhere all over the school. Her highest concern is with the quality of the instructional program, and that is the topic of most of her conversations with teachers. She has managed to gain the collective commitment of her staff to strive for excellence and to expend whatever energies it takes to get there.

McGary and her staff have shown themselves to be open to ideas and suggestions from anywhere, so long as they produce results. For example, one of her teachers had worked in the Marva Collins School in Chicago, which was known for its high performance. It was a private school that sent virtually all of its students to college, though they came from the urban areas of Chicago. McGary saw that this teacher could be a resource, not only for students but for other faculty members as well.

After one year of operation, the teachers at Harmony-Leland with whom I spoke were brimming with pride. Overworked and underpaid, they exuded a sense of mission. Visitors I refer to Harmony-Leland see that this is a very different place from most urban schools. It is different in terms of the expectations that teachers have of students. Although Harmony-Leland has been able to achieve these results in its later stages with some assistance, at the beginning it proved its ability to help students to achieve before the resources came.

It is a clear insult to those who work as hard as Sandra McGary, her key leadership staff, and the teachers, with the support of parents, to attribute the success of Harmony-Leland School to "charisma." There is no doubt that McGary is highly charismatic. However, that merely serves to energize the faculty and staff, causing them to apply those energies to time on task. It is the hard work and sweat and tears of the principal and teachers that account for the excellent outcomes for students. The charisma is a bonus.

There are several schools within my collection of high-achieving schools where no special charisma is to be found. Ordinary teachers and ordinary principals with extraordinary commitment and energies can transform ordinary schools, and even failing schools, into islands of hope in a sea of despair. When I first came to Atlanta in 1980, the Dunbar Elementary School was a school much like Harmony-Leland, a school that had transformed itself from one of the worst-performing schools in Atlanta to the highest, in spite of being located in Carver Homes, a very low-income neighborhood at the time. My visit to the Dunbar School, and my conversation with its principal, revealed the relaxed way in which the faculty had gone about producing this high achievement. The principal told me that she simply confronted her faculty and told them that she did not know how to get the excellent achievement that she knew was possible with their students, but that she had great faith that if given the time to collaborate, the faculty could solve the problem of how to do that, and then she turned away and held them accountable for creating the solutions that did indeed raise Dunbar School to levels of excellence.

It is this process that fascinates me and that seems to explain McGary and the Harmony-Leland better than most of the models professional educators use to describe schools. It is the human beings, the principals and the teachers who have the innate capacity to solve problems, who can change schools without functioning like zombies or robots. It is leadership that can help to create an environment within which the creative potential of teachers can be released. McGary gave a great deal of direction to her faculty and staff. At the same time, she gave a great deal of latitude to her teachers to apply themselves to the task of creating a powerful learning environment for students. Her approach worked; the teachers found a way through collaborative problem solving.

One of my greatest worries is that the popular models of "school reform" reflect a popular understanding about approaches to teaching and learning that reduce the professionals in schools to inhuman respondents to bureaucratic dictates. Courageous leaders like Sandra McGary make their own pathways because they have the confidence that a path can be made. She and other such principals are joined by their faculties in a creative problem-solving quest. The difference between these schools and others where teachers await their assignments, even micromanaging assignments, is the difference between joy and despair. I fear not only for the teachers in despair; I fear for the experiences of students who are served by despairing teachers. Good leaders lift their teachers up.

Other kinds of accounts of whole school environments where children achieve at consistently high levels are available. Alan Peshkin (2001) has written an exciting book, *Permissible Advantage,* that provides us with a fresh and unusual opportunity to look at the question of savage inequalities in a more precise way. We can see clearly from this book that the quality of service, and consequent opportunity to learn, is the true explanation for the achievement gap. Peshkin's report on the elite Edgewood Academy in New Mexico is a description of how schools work when they have all of the resources they need and when their leaders have a mission to educate and socialize students for positions of power. Examining the experience of children in the enriched experience at Edgewood Academy with an outstanding faculty, trained and selected to provide towering academic achievement and achieving that result, allows us to see clearly that nothing remotely resembling the Edgewood Academy experience has ever been made available to the masses of poor African children.

Moving these children's performance to levels of excellence may not even require all the advantages that wealth can bestow. In fact, public education in regular schools, and even private education at a fraction of the cost of Edgewood, has been able to produce extraordinary results with African students. However, we still need to look closely at how very wealthy people educate their children, in places where educators do not have the same conversations that tend to be held in schools that serve low-income African students. This is a neglected area in educational research. Because the details are lost to educational research by the absence of more close ethnographies of elite schools, we lose the opportunity to understand at a deeper level exactly what the nature of the quality of service is that we provide to our students, compared with those at schools like Edgewood Academy.

WHAT TO DO: THE FAILURE OF
THE PUBLIC POLICY PARADIGM

Among many other things, the accounts of gap-closing environments above show that public policy, ostensibly designed to transform schools and to make them places where there are indeed opportunities to learn, is often misguided. Among the myriad misguided policies and reforms common in education today are manipulating test score requirements in high-stakes testing, using school vouchers, using school charters, purchasing commercial programs, bureaucratizing parts of the educational process, especially remedial and special education, in order to respond to children's needs, such as the Individual Education Plan team assessment and micromanagement of the instructional process and nonspecial special education. Each of these practices, which together constitute the virtual totality of our response to low performance of African children, is fundamentally flawed. Although testing may introduce a measure of accountability, "weighing the elephant" will not make it grow. Although vouchers might offer some children options that could be beneficial in public policy proposals, the voucher trick offers a fraction of the cost of a private education to dupe students who leave public education without any documentation of beneficial outcomes for such a move. Charters may work, but they are not a universal reform tool for students who are not fortunate enough to be a part of a particular charter, especially a high-quality charter. Almost without exception, centralized bureaucratic regulations and accountability activities set in motion things that, though well meaning, have no record whatsoever of offering benefits to students. And finally, special education is not special.

Popular public policy proposals are pitiful as means to change things in substantial and positive ways for the masses of our children, and for African children in general.

In general, educators have pursued what I call "decoy issues," such as the testing issue, the preoccupation with the child capacity issue, and the "reform issue." None of them captures the essence of what I have attempted to discuss above, and that is to adopt an approach that encourages high-quality teaching. We need a major effort at describing the nature of services currently provided. This information would become a management tool, allowing for leadership decisions to be made about staff development, assignment, supervision, and rewards. Such an alliance of research and policy is not in operation at this time for the simple reason that our paradigm for thinking about schools is flawed fundamentally. We are doing what J. Arthur Jones warned against in his critique of Eleanor Orr. We focus most of our attention on the children and little on the quality of service and equity in its distribution.

Colleges of education have the opportunity to produce outstanding teachers and outstanding school leaders. In a few cases, they already do. But I want schools of education to turn out gap-closing principals and gap-closing teachers. It is unlikely that such gap-closing production can occur in the absence of a gap-closing teacher education faculty, particularly the faculty in charge of the clinical experience for teachers and school leaders. Yes, it takes a gap closer to teach a gap closer!

What we find in teacher education is a parallel to what we find with students. Brilliant teachers come to the university, but in teacher education, few have the opportunity to learn from gap closers. As a result, they may take false learned notions into the field, such as those doubts about capacity discussed above, which in many ways come straight out of the teacher education curriculum. They may become confused about their own instincts about teaching and learning, some of which are correct but not nourished. But above all, they lose the opportunity to be inspired by the best of their profession in the interest of children. This must change. In order for it to change, serious examination must be made of gap-closing professional education. Like gap-closing teaching, gap-closing teacher education and gap-closing education leadership is already in operation, though it is not typical. Our challenge is to make this excellence typical.

THE AFRICAN EXCELLENCE TRADITION IN EDUCATION:
A FOUNDATION FOR UNDERSTANDING WHO AFRICANS
ARE AND SOURCES OF VALID PEDAGOGY

I want to say a brief word about what African people have brought to America. Many misguided ideas about the education of African people have emerged and persist, in large part because of our ignorance of who African people are. This ignorance also exists among African people themselves, many of whom have forgotten who they are, or who missed the intergenerational cultural transmission that should have been offered. To know the cultural wealth that African people brought, especially in the areas of education, is to transform opinions and images of the intellectual capacities of African people. There is an ancient deep well of cultural resources, especially in teaching and learning, including higher education, that could improve the education of Africans and others. The Africa that most Americans know is a cruel caricature of its historical reality. A robust literature is available to correct the negative and distorted picture.

Few educators are aware of this history and tradition because of the "iron curtain" at the national borders that prevents us from seeing African behavior on the continent, and because of the "iron curtain in time" that prevents us from seeing African behavior anywhere before 1492. This is the period of the beginning of slavery, colonization, and the apartheid/segregation and the ideology of white supremacy, and its impact on African people worldwide. Few educators know that there were three Nile Valley centers of higher education in Africa before European or other penetration into the continent—in ancient Kemet, in two centers in Kush, Nubia, and Ethiopia. Few educators know that there were major Niger Valley centers of higher education. Both traditional and new. On the Niger River, there was the university town of Timbuktu and the Dogon traditional university systems in Mali. There was the Sokoto Empire in Nigeria as well as the Congo higher education systems. There were other higher educational systems throughout Africa. The fragments that allow us to document these experiences are being uncovered daily from archeological and text records, in addition to existing continuities of old systems that are little changed from ancient times.

There is now literature that leads us in the right places, but our questions have to take us there. Enslaved Africans continued these systems on these plantations under the noses of their masters, as reported by Thomas Webber (1978) in *Deep Like the River.* With the emancipation of Africans from slavery in America, there was an explosive growth of self-determination in schooling, and this schooling was highly successful, as reported by James Anderson (1988). Multilingual Africans came to America and continued their genius for language in Maroon societies and as interpreters for the military. Finally, this awesome African literary tradition is now being documented. An examination of that literature alone will show to African people and to other interested people intellectual and cultural wealth beyond the imagination. These things should be made available to enhance the experience of African students and to enlighten the world about African people.

The references above will lead to materials that are arresting, unexpected, vital, and relevant to education today, as they paint a picture of the genius, humanity, and spirituality of African people. Our present education system conveys little to no sense of these things. In fact, through omission and distortion, our curriculum and treatment of African children tends to make matters worse year by year, alienating African people from themselves and alienating the traditions of Africa from the mainstream of world civilization.

J. S. Chick School in Kansas City, Missouri, is a public African-centered school, a school that teaches the children about their heritage, reintroducing many to their traditional ways.

According to the LINK Commissioner Report, published by the Kansas City public schools, in 2002 "Chick scored higher on the MAP [Missouri Assessment Program] test than any other school in the Kansas City, Mo., School District." This is a very important demonstration of the fact that there is no conflict between having an African-centered school and having excellent performance on standardized achievement. Resisting educators and policy makers frequently make a false dichotomy when parents and communities demand culturally salient schools. Chick and other African-centered public and private schools demonstrate that children can do "both and," and there is no reason to choose "either or." We owe each child a curriculum that does not glorify others at the expense of a curriculum of inclusion. In an article in the *New York Times,* Edward Wong examines a recent report from the Department of Education:

> The report . . . examined six federal programs, including the Title I program that allocates $8 billion each year to try to help disadvantaged children get access to teachers and computers. The report was based on data from the 1997–1998 school year collected in 720 schools in 180 districts.
>
> The report showed that although secondary schools had a third of the country's more impoverished students, only 15 percent of Title I money went to those schools.
>
> One of the report's more disturbing findings showed that teachers' aids rather than qualified teachers were teaching many students in Title I schools.
>
> Although almost all of the teacher's aides in Title I schools had a high school diploma or an equivalent degree, only 19 percent had a bachelor's degree, the report said. That figure dropped to 10 percent in the schools with the highest poverty rates.
>
> Half of the instructional workers supported by Title I money were teachers' aides, but 41 percent of these aides said that they spent at least half of their time teaching students on their own, without a teacher present.
>
> While federal money paid for almost a quarter of the computers that schools received in the 1997–1998 school year, "high-poverty schools had less access to technology than low-poverty schools in terms of the quality, quantity and connectivity of computers," the report said. (Wong 2000)

Clearly, the issue is the quality of instruction!!!

J. Arthur Jones was right. It is the quality of teaching and not questions about the capacity of children that must carry the weight of our attention. One of the real problems that we face is the seeming inability of some educators to receive important information about school power and teacher power. Time and time again, documentation of the power of teaching and of schools has been presented. If we really care about the children, news like that will be received and appropriate actions taken to learn as much as possible about the source of the successes. We will see that our fundamental policy problem is the quality of teacher education.

We must ask, who are the teacher educators and school leadership educators who produce the teachers and leaders who produce success? There should be no other kind. Virtually any teacher or school leader can be taught how to be as successful as the educators who have been mentioned above. There is no mystery about how to do this, any more than there is a mystery about how to get high achievement from any child.

We would have to admit that the vast majority of teachers and school leaders have not been given what they should have been given. Many of us cannot bear the thought of going through another round of training. Rightfully, we are suspicious that any new round of teacher education is likely to be no better that what we have already endured.

However, we cannot continue to do what we have always done, just because it is too costly to do something different in our training program. We need only copy the many educators who have long track records of teaching teachers and school leaders how to be success-ful. When teachers and educational leaders do find power powerful teacher education and school leadership education, it has been my ex-perience that they are more than willing to make sacrifices to become the masters of their craft that they can become.

The successful teachers and school leaders should be the new school leaders. There is no place in educational leadership for puzzled leaders. Those for whom the path to success is no mystery must lead us.

If we love the children, then we must do whatever it takes to pro-vide them with the teachers and school leaders they deserve. We cannot tolerate or support ideologies and practices that cripple our children further—those that hold that our children are the problem or those that assume that our teachers and school leaders are not capa-ble of becoming powerful factors in the lives of students. We need a valid vision. We need the will. With vision and will, everything is possible.

Ronald Edmonds was right: "We can, whenever and wherever we wish, teach successfully all children whose education is of interest to us. Whether we do or do not do it depends in the final analysis on how we feel about the fact that we have not done so thus far." This says in the strongest way that it is a matter of will. Do we really want the Afri-can children to be excellent? If so, there is no mystery about how to make that happen.

REFERENCES

Perry / Up from the Parched Earth: Toward a Theory of
African-American Achievement

Anderson, James. 1988. *The Education of Blacks in the South, 1860–1935*. Chapel Hill:
University of North Carolina Press.

Angelou, Maya. 1969. *I Know Why the Caged Bird Sings*. New York: Random House.

Au, Kathryn Hu-Pei. 1980. "Participation Structures in a Reading Lesson with
Hawaiian Children." *Anthropology and Education Quarterly* 11: 91–115.

Baldwin, James. 1979. "If Black English Isn't a Language Then Tell Me What Is It?"
New York Times, July 29.

———. 1984. "African Self-Consciousness and the Mental Health of African-
Americans." *Journal of Black Studies* 15 (2): 177–94.

———. 1985. *The Price of the Ticket: Collected Nonfiction, 1948–1985*. New York: St.
Martin's.

Ballenger, C. 1997. "Social Identities, Moral Narratives, Scientific Argumentation:
Science Talk in a Bilingual Classroom." *Language and Education* 11(1): 1–14.

Benjamin, Lois. 1991. *The Black Elite: Facing the Color Line in the Twilight of the Twentieth Century*. Chicago: Nelson Hall.

Bourdieu, Pierre. 1970. "Cultural Reproduction and Social Reproduction." British
Sociological Conference.

———. 1984. *Distinctions: The Social Critique of the Judgement of Taste*. Cambridge:
Harvard University Press.

Bourdieu, Pierre, and Jean-Claude Passeron. 1977. *Reproduction in Education, Society,
and Culture*. Trans. Richard Nice. Beverly Hills: Sage.

Bowman, Philip, and Cleopatra Howard. 1985. "Race-Related Socialization,
Motivation, and Academic Achievement: A Study of Black Youth in Three-
Generation Families." *Journal of the American Academy of Child Psychiatry* 24:
134–41.

Boykin, A. Wade, and Forrest D. Toms. 1985. "Black Child Socialization: A Conceptual Framework." In *Black Children: Social, Educational, and Parental Environments,* ed. H. P. McAdoo and J. L. McAdoo. Beverly Hills: Sage.

Bullock, Henry Allen. 1967. *A History of Negro Education in the South from 1614 to the
Present*. Cambridge: Harvard University Press.

Butchart, Ronald E. 1980. *Northern Schools, Southern Blacks, and Reconstruction: Freedom's Education, 1862–1875*. Westport, Conn.: Greenwood.

Carson, Benjamin S., and Cecil Murphey. 1990. *Gifted Hands: The Ben Carson Story*.
New York: Zondervan.

Cazden, Courtney B., Vera P. John, and Dell Hymes, eds. 1972. *The Function of Language in the Classroom*. New York: Teachers College.

Clark, Septima. 1990. *Ready from Within: Septima Clark and the Civil Rights Movement*. Edited and with an introduction by Cynthia Stokes Brown. Trenton: Africa World.

College Board. 1999. *Reaching the Top: A Report of the National Task Force on Minority High Achievement*. New York: College Board.

Conant, F. 1996. "Drums in the Science Lab." *Hands On* 19(1): 7–10.

Cornelius, Janet Duitsman. 1991. *When I Can Read My Title Clear: Literacy, Slavery, and Religion in the Antebellum South*. Columbia: University of South Carolina Press.

Crouch, Stanley. 1993. "Who Are We? Where Did We Come From? Where Are We Going?" In *Lure and Loathing: Essays on Race, Identity, and the Ambivalence of Assimilation,* ed. Gerald Early. New York: Allen Lane-Penguin.

Dates, Janette L., and William Barlow. 1990. *Split Image: African Americans in the Mass Media*. Washington, D.C.: Howard University Press.

Davis, Charles T., and Henry Louis Gates, eds. 1990. *Slave Narratives*. Oxford: Oxford University Press.

Delpit, Lisa. 1993. "The Politics of Teaching Literate Discourse." In *Freedom's Plow: Teaching in the Multicultural Classroom,* ed. Theresa Perry and James Fraser. New York: Routledge.

———. 1995. *Other People's Children*. New York: Free Press.

Delpit, Lisa, and Joanne Kilgour Dowdy, eds. 2002. *The Skin That We Speak: Thoughts on Language and Culture in the Classroom*. New York: New Press.

DiMaggio, Paul. 1982. "Cultural Capital and School Success: The Impact of Status Culture Participation on the Grades of U.S. High School Students." *American Sociological Review* 47: 189–201.

Douglass, Frederick. 1968. *The Narrative of the Life of Frederick Douglass: An American Slave*. New York: Signet.

Drewry, Henry N., Humphrey Doermann, and Susan Anderson. 2001. *Stand and Prosper: Private Black Colleges and Their Students*. Princeton, N.J.: Princeton University Press.

Du Bois, W. E. B. 1903. "The Talented Tenth." In *The Negro Problem: A Series of Articles by Representative Negroes of Today,* ed. Booker T. Washington. New York: Pott and Co.

———. 1989. *The Souls of Black Folk*. New York: Penguin.

Early, Gerald, ed. 1993. *Lure and Loathing: Essays on Race, Identity, and the Ambivalence of Assimilation*. New York: Allen Lane-Penguin.

Edwards, Audrey, and Craig K. Polite. 1992. *Children of the Dream: The Psychology of Black Success*. New York: Doubleday.

Elders, Joycelyn, and David Chanoff. 1996. *Joycelyn Elders, M.D.: From Sharecropper's Daughter to Surgeon General of the United States of America*. New York: William Morrow.

Ellison, Ralph. 1972. *Shadow and Act*. New York: Vintage Books.

Erickson, Frederick. 1987. "Transformation and School Success: The Politics and Culture of Educational Achievement." *Anthropology and Education* 18 (4): 335–56.

Essed, Philomena. 1991. *Understanding Everyday Racism: An Interdisciplinary Theory.* Newbury Park: Sage.

Fairclough, Adam. 2001. *Teaching Equality: Black Schools in the Age of Jim Crow.* Athens: University of Georgia Press.

Fields, Barbara. 1982. "Ideology and Race in American History." In *Region, Race and Reconstruction,* ed. J. Morgan Kousser and James McPherson. New York: Oxford University Press.

Foley, D. E. 1991. "Reconsidering Anthropological Explanations of Ethnic School Failure." *Anthropology and Education Quarterly* 22: 60–85.

Foner, Philip S., and Robert James Branham, eds. 1998. *Lift Every Voice: African American Oratory, 1787–1900.* Tuscaloosa: University of Alabama Press.

Fordham, Signithia. 1986. *Black Student School Success: An Ethnographic Study in a Large Urban Public School System.* New York: Spencer Foundation.

———. 1988. "Racelessness as a Factor in Black Students' School Success: Pragmatic Strategy or Pyrrhic Victory?" *Harvard Educational Review* 58 (1): 54–84.

Fordham, Signithia, and John Ogbu. 1986. "Black Students' School Success: Coping with the 'Burden of "Acting White." ' " *Urban Review* 18 (3): 176–206.

Gutman, Herbert. 1976. *The Black Family in Slavery and Freedom, 1750–1925.* New York: Pantheon.

Heath, S. B. 1982. "Questioning at Home and at School: A Comparative Study." In *Doing the Ethnography of Schooling: Educational Anthropology in Action,* ed. George Spindler, pp. 102–31. New York: Holt, Rinehart, and Winston.

———. 1983. *Ways with Words: Language, Life, and Work in Communities and Classrooms.* Cambridge: Cambridge University Press.

Holland, Dorothy, William Lachicotte, Debra Skinner, and Carole Cain. 1998. *Identity and Agency in Cultural Worlds.* Cambridge: Harvard University Press.

Hrabowski, Freeman A., Kenneth I. Maton, Geoffrey L. Greif. 1998. *Beating the Odds: Raising Academically Successful African American Males.* New York: Oxford University Press.

Hrabowski, Freeman A., Kenneth I. Maton, Geoffrey L. Greif, and Monica L. Greene. 2002. *Overcoming the Odds: Raising Academically Successful African American Young Women.* New York: Oxford University Press.

Huggins, Nathan. 1971. *Harlem Renaissance.* New York: Oxford University Press.

Ignatiev, Noel. 1995. *How the Irish Became White.* New York: Routledge.

Jacobs, Harriet. 1987. *Incidents in the Life of a Slave Girl.* Ed. Jean Fagan Yellin. Cambridge: Harvard University Press.

Johnson, James Weldon. 1912. *The Autobiography of an Ex-Colored Man.* Boston: Sherman, French.

Jones-Wilson, Faustine C. 1981. *A Traditional Model of Educational Excellence: Dunbar High School of Little Rock, Arkansas.* Washington, D.C.: Howard University Press.

Kochman, Thomas. 1981. *Black and White: Styles in Conflict.* Chicago: University of Chicago Press.

Labov, William. 1972a. *Language in the Inner City: Studies in the Black English Vernacular.* Philadelphia: University of Pennsylvania Press.

———. 1972b. *Sociolinguistic Patterns.* Philadelphia: University of Pennsylvania Press.

Ladson-Billings, G. 1994. *The Dreamkeepers: Successful Teachers of African American Children.* San Francisco: Jossey-Bass.

Ledbetter, James. 1992. "Imitation of Life." *Vibe Magazine,* fall, 112–14.

Lee, C. 1993. *Signifying as a Scaffold of Genre.* Urbana, Ill.: National Council of Teachers of English.

Lee, Spike, dir. 1989. *Do the Right Thing.* Perf. Paul Benjamin. Videocassette. Universal.

Lynk, Miles V. 1896. *The Afro American School Speaker and Gems of Literature.* Jackson, Tenn.

Malcolm X. 1975. *The Autobiography of Malcolm X.* New York: Random House.

Mathis, Deborah. 2002. *Yet a Stranger: Why Black Americans Still Don't Feel at Home.* New York: Warner.

McClain, Leanita. 1986. *A Foot in Each World.* Evanston, Ill.: Northwestern University Press.

Morin, Laraine, Linda Mizell, Susan Bennett, and Bisse Bowman. 1993. "Different Ways of Seeing: Teaching in an Anti-Racist School." In *Freedom's Plow: Teaching in the Multicultural Classroom,* ed. Theresa Perry and James Fraser. New York: Routledge.

Morrison, Toni. 1989a. *Playing in the Dark: Whiteness and the Literary Imagination.* Cambridge: Harvard University Press.

———. 1989b. "Unspeakable Things Unspoken: The Afro-American Presence in American Literature." *Michigan Quarterly Review* 28: 1–34.

Murray, Pauli. 1978. *Proud Shoes: The Story of an African American Family.* New York: Harper & Row.

Ogbu, John. 1981a. "Black Education: A Cultural-Ecological Perspective." In *Black Families,* ed. H. P. McAdoo, pp. 139–54. Beverly Hills: Sage.

———. 1981b. "Origins of Human Competence: A Cultural-Ecological Perspective." *Child Development* 52: 413–29.

———. 1981c. "Schooling in the Ghetto: An Ecological Perspective on Community and Home Influences." National Institution of Education Follow-Through Planning Conferences, Philadelphia.

———. 1983. "Minority Status and Schooling in Plural Societies." *Comparative Education Review* 27 (2): 168–90.

Parker, Gwendolyn. 1997. *Trespassing: My Sojourn in the Halls of Privilege.* Boston: Houghton Mifflin.

Perry, Theresa. 1982. *Towards an Interpretive Analysis of the Martin Luther King v. Ann Arbor School Board Case.* Unpublished manuscript.

Perry, Theresa, and Lisa Delpit, eds. 1998. *The Real Ebonics Debate: Power, Language, and the Education of African-American Children.* Boston: Beacon.

Pierce, Chester. 1989. "Unity in Diversity: Thirty-three Years of Stress." In *Black Students: Psychosocial Issues and Academic Achievement,* ed. G. L. Berry and J. K. Asamen, pp. 296–312. Newbury Park, Calif.: Sage.

Prager, Jeffrey. 1982. "American Racial Ideology as Collective Representation." *Ethnic and Racial Studies* 5 (1): 99–119.

Rawick, George. 1972. *From Sundown to Sunup: The Making of the Black Community.* Westport, Conn.: Greenwood.

Richards, Judith. 1993. "Classroom Tapestry: A Practitioner's Perspective on Multicultural Education." In *Freedom's Plow: Teaching in the Multicultural Classroom,* ed. Theresa Perry and James Fraser. New York: Routledge.

Roediger, David. 1991. *The Wages of Whiteness.* London: Verso.

———. 1993. "The White Question." *Race Traitor* 1 (winter): 104–7.

Scott, James. 1990. *Domination and the Arts of Resistance.* New Haven, Conn. Yale University Press.

Scott, Joyce H. 1979. *Integrated Classroom: A Paradox of Equal Opportunity? A Study of the Role of the Black Teacher in Segregated and Integrated Settings.* Boston: Boston University School of Education.

Scott, Kesho Yvonne. *The Habit of Surviving: Black Women's Strategies for Life.* New Brunswick, N.J.: Rutgers University Press, 1991.

Siu, Sau-Fong. 1992. *Toward an Understanding of Chinese-American Educational Achievement: A Literature Review.* Boston: Center on Families, Communities, Schools, and Children's Learning.

Smith, Roland. 1995. "Building Community, Raising Expectations, Creating Scholars: The Xavier University Experience." American Educational Research Association Meeting, San Francisco.

Sowell, Thomas. 1974. "Black Excellence: The Case of Dunbar High School." *Public Interest* 35: 1–21.

———. 1976. "Patterns of Black Excellence." *Public Interest* 43: 26–58.

Stepto, Robert B. 1991. *From Behind the Veil: A Study of Afro-American Narrative.* Urbana: University of Illinois Press.

Walker, Vanessa Siddle. 1996. *Their Highest Potential: An African American School Community in the Segregated South.* Chapel Hill: University of North Carolina Press.

Ward, Janie Victoria. 1991. *Eyes in the Back of Your Head: Moral Themes in African American Narratives of Racial Conflict.* Unpublished manuscript.

Waters, Mary C. 1999. *Black Identities: West Indian Immigrant Dreams and American Realities.* Cambridge: Harvard University Press.

Webber, Thomas L. 1978. *Deep Like the Rivers: Education in the Slave Quarter Community, 1831–1865.* New York: Norton.

Weinberg, Meyer. 1977. *A Chance to Learn: A History of Race and Education in the United States.* Cambridge: Cambridge University Press.

West, Cornel. 1997. *Restoring Hope: Conversations on the Future of Black America.* Ed. Kelvin Shawn Sealey. Boston: Beacon.

White, J. L., and T. A. Parham. 1990. *The Psychology of Blacks: An African American Perspective,* 2nd ed. Englewood Cliffs: Prentice Hall.

Wright, Richard. 1937. *Black Boy.* New York: Harper & Row.

———. 1968. "The Ethics of Living Jim Crow: An Autobiographical Sketch." In *Black Voices,* ed. Abraham Chapman. New York: New American Library.

Steele / Stereotype Threat and African-American Student Achievement

Abrams, D., and M. A. Hogg. 1999. *Social Identity and Social Cognition.* Malden, Mass.: Blackwell.

Allport, G. 1954. *The Nature of Prejudice.* New York: Addison-Wesley.

Ambady, N., M. Shih, A. Kim, and T. L. Pittinsky. 2001. "Stereotype Susceptibility in Children: Effects of Identity Activation on Quantitative Performance." *Psychological Science* 12: 385–90.

Aronson, J. 1997. *The Effects of Conceptions of Ability on Task Valuation.* Unpublished manuscript, New York University.

———. 1999. *The Effects of Conceiving Ability as Fixed or Improvable on Responses to Stereotype Threat.* Unpublished manuscript, New York University.

Aronson, J., C. Fried, and C. Good. 2002. "Reducing the Effects of Stereotype Threat on African American College Students by Shaping Theories of Intelligence." *Journal of Experimental Social Psychology* 38: 113–25.

Aronson, J., and C. Good. 2001. *Personal versus Situational Stakes and Stereotype Threat: A test of the Vanguard Hypothesis.* Manuscript in preparation, New York University.

Aronson, J., M. Lustina, C. Good, K. Keough, C. Steele, and J. Brown. 1999. "When White Men Can't Do Math: Necessary and Sufficient Factors in Stereotype Threat." *Journal of Experimental Social Psychology* 35: 29–46.

Aronson, J., D. M. Quinn, and S. J. Spencer. 1998. "Stereotype Threat and the Academic Performance of Women and Minorities." In *Prejudice: The Target's Perspective,* ed. J. K. Swim and C. Stangor, pp. 83–103. San Diego, Calif.: Academic Press.

Aronson, J., and M. F. Salinas. 2001. *Stereotype Threat, Attributional Ambiguity, and Latino Underperformance.* Unpublished manuscript, New York University.

Ashe, A. 1993. *Days of Grace.* New York: Knopf.

Bargh, J. A., M. Chen, and L. Burrows. 1996. "Automaticity of Social Behavior: Direct Effects of Trait Construct and Stereotype Activation on Action." *Journal of Personality and Social Psychology* 71: 230–44.

Benbow, C. P., and J. C. Stanley. 1983. "Sex Differences in Mathematical Reasoning Ability: More Facts." *Science* 222: 1029–31.

Blascovich, J., S. J. Spencer, D. M. Quinn, and C. M. Steele. 2001. "Stereotype

Threat and the Cardiovascular Reactivity of African-Americans." *Psychological Science* 12: 225–29.

Bowen, W. G., and D. C. Bok. 1998. *The Shape of the River: Long-Term Consequences of Considering Race in College and University Admissions.* Princeton, N.J.: Princeton University Press.

Branscombe, N. R., and N. Ellemers. 1998. "Coping with Group-Based Discrimination: Individualistic versus Group-Level Strategies." In *Prejudice: The Target's Perspective,* ed. J. K. Swim and C. Stangor, pp. 243–66. San Diego, Calif.: Academic Press.

Brewer, M. B., and R. B. Brown. 1998. "Intergroup Relations." In *The Handbook of Social Psychology,* 4th ed. Vol. 2, ed. D. T. Gilbert, S. T. Fiske, and G. Lindzey, pp. 554–94. Boston: McGraw-Hill.

Brown, J. L., and C. M. Steele. 2001. *Performance Expectations Are Not a Necessary Mediator of Stereotype Threat in African American Verbal Test Performance.* Unpublished manuscript, Stanford University.

Brown, R. P., and R. A. Josephs. 1999. "A Burden of Proof: Stereotype Relevance and Gender Differences in Math Performance." *Journal of Personality and Social Psychology* 76: 246–57.

Brown, R. P., E. C. Pinel, P. Rentfrow, and M. Lee. 2001. *Stigma on My Mind: Individual Differences in the Experience of Stereotype Threat.* Unpublished Manuscript, University of Oklahoma.

Cohen, G. L., C. M. Steele, and L. D. Ross. 1999. "The Mentors' Dilemma: Providing Critical Feedback across the Racial Time." *Personality and Social Psychology Bulletin* 25: 1302–18.

Cole, S., and E. Barber. 2000. *Increasing Faculty Diversity: The Occupational Choices of High Achieving Minority Students.* A report prepared for the Council of Ivy Group Presidents.

Crocker, J., and B. Major. 1989. "Social Stigma and Self-Esteem: The Self-Protective Properties of Stigma." *Psychological Review* 96: 608–30.

Crocker, J., B. Major, and C. Steele. 1998. "Social Stigma." In *The Handbook of Social Psychology,* 4th ed. Vol. 2, ed. D. T. Gilbert, S. T. Fiske, and G. Lindzey, pp. 504–53. Boston: McGraw-Hill.

Crocker, J., K. Voelkl, M. Testa, and B. Major. 1991. "Social Stigma: The Affective Consequences of Attributional Ambiguity." *Journal of Personality and Social Psychology* 60: 218–28.

Croizet, J. C., and T. Claire. 1998. "Extending the Concept of Stereotype Threat to Social Class: The Intellectual Underperformance of Students from Low Socioeconomic Backgrounds." *Personality and Social Psychology Bulletin* 24: 588–94.

Crosby, F. J. 1984. "The Denial of Personal Discrimination." *American Behavioral Scientist* 27: 371–86.

Crosby, F. J., D. I. Cordova, and K. Jaskar. 1993. "On the Failure to See Oneself as Disadvantaged: Cognitive and Emotional Components." In *Group Motivation:*

Social Psychological Perspectives, ed. M. A. Hogg, and D. Abrams, pp. 87–104. Hertfordshire, England: Harvester Wheatsheaf.

Cross, W. E., Jr. 1991. *Shades of Black: Diversity in African-American Identity.* Philadelphia: Temple University Press.

Davies, P. G., and S. J. Spencer. 1999. *Selling Stereotypes: How Viewing Commercials Can Undermine Women's Math Performance.* Presented at the annual meeting of the American Psychological Association. Boston, August.

————. 2001. *Stereotype Threat and Taking Charge: The Effect of Demeaning Commercials on Women's Leadership Aspirations.* Unpublished manuscript, Stanford University.

Davies, P. G., S. J. Spencer, D. M. Quinn, and R. Gerhardstein. 2001. *Consuming Images: How Television Commercials That Elicit Stereotype Threat Can Restrain Women Academically and Professionally.* Unpublished manuscript, Stanford University.

Deaux, K., and B. Major. 1987. "Putting Gender into Context: An Interactive Model of Gender-Related Behavior." *Psychological Review* 94: 369–89.

Devine, P. G. 1989. "Stereotypes and Prejudice: Their Automatic and Controlled Components." *Journal of Personality and Social Psychology* 56: 5–18.

Dweck, C. S., C. Chiu, and Y. Hong. 1995. "Implicit Theories and Their Role in Judgments and Reactions: A World from Two Perspectives." *Psychological Inquiry* 6: 267–85.

Folkman, S., R. S. Lazarus, R. J. Gruen, and A. DeLongis. 1986. "Appraisal, Coping, Health Status, and Psychological Symptoms." *Journal of Personality and Social Psychology* 50: 571–79.

Goffman, I. 1963. *Stigma.* New York: Simon & Schuster.

Good, C., and J. Aronson. (In press). "The Development and Consequences of Stereotype Vulnerability in Adolescents." In *Adolescence and Education.* Vol. 2, *Academic Motivation of Adolescents,* ed. F. Pajares, and T. Urdan. Greenwich, Conn.: Information Age Publishing.

Good, C., J. Aronson, and J. A. Harder. 2001. *Stereotype Threat in the Absence of a Kernel of Truth: Unfounded Stereotypes Can Depress Women's Calculus Performance.* Unpublished manuscript, Columbia University.

Graham, C., R. W. Baker, and S. Wapner. 1984. "Prior Interracial Experience and Black Student Transition into Predominantly White Colleges." *Journal of Personality and Social Psychology* 47: 1146–54.

Inzlicht, M., and T. Ben-Zeev. 2000. "A Threatening Intellectual Environment: Why Females Are Susceptible to Experiencing Problem-Solving Deficits in the Presence of Males." *Psychological Science* 11: 365–71.

Jensen, A. R. 1980. *Bias in Mental Testing.* New York: Free Press.

Jonides, J., W. von Hippel, J. S. Lerner, and B. Nagda. 1992. *Evaluation of Minority Retention Programs: The Undergraduate Research Opportunities Program at the University of Michigan.* Presented at the annual meeting of the American Psychological Association. Washington, D.C., August.

Josephs, R. A., M. L. Newman, R. P. Brown, and J. M. Beer. 2001. *Using the Relation-*

ship between Status and Testosterone to Explain Stereotype-Based Sex Differences in Cognitive Performance. Unpublished manuscript, University of Texas.

Jost, J. T., and M. R. Banaji. 1994. "The Role of Stereotyping in System-Justification and the Production of False Consciousness." *British Journal of Social Psychology Special Issue: Stereotypes: Structure, Function, and Process* 33: 1–27.

Kleck, R. E., and A. Strenta. 1980. "Perceptions of the Impact of Negatively Valued Physical Characteristics on Social Interaction." *Journal of Personality and Social Psychology* 39: 861–73.

Lazarus, R. S. 1986. "Emotions and Adaption: Conceptual and Empirical Relations." *Nebraska Symposium on Motivation* 16: 175–266.

Lepper, M. R., M. Woolverton, D. L. Mumme, and J. L. Gurtner. 1993. "Motivational Techniques of Expert Human Tutors: Lessons for the Design of Computer-Based Tutors." In *Computers as Cognitive Tools: Technology in Education,* ed. S. P. Lajoie, and S. J. Derry. Hillsdale, N.J.: Lawrence Erlbaum.

Leyens, J. P., M. Désert, J. C. Croizet, and C. Darcis. 2000. "Stereotype Threat: Are Lower Status and History of Stigmatization Preconditions of Stereotype Threat?" *Personality and Social Psychology Bulletin* 26: 1189–99.

Macrae, C. N., G. V. Bodenhausen, A. B. Milne, and J. Jetten. 1994. "Out of Mind but Back in Sight: Stereotypes on the Rebound." *Journal of Personality and Social Psychology* 67: 808–17.

Major, B. 1995. *Academic Performance, Self-Esteem, and Race: The Role of Disidentification.* Presented at the annual meeting of the American Psychological Association. New York, August.

Major, B., and T. Schmader. 1998. "Coping with Stigma through Psychological Disengagement." In *Prejudice: The Target's Perspective,* ed. J. K. Swim, and C. Stangor, pp. 219–41. San Diego, Calif.: Academic Press.

Major, B., S. J. Spencer, T. Schmader, C. T. Wolfe, and J. Crocker. 1998. "Coping with Negative Stereotypes about Intellectual Performance: The Role of Psychological Disengagement." *Personality and Social Psychology Bulletin* 24: 34–50.

Markus, H. R., C. M. Steele, and D. M. Steele. 2000. "Colorblindness as a Barrier to Inclusion: Assimilation and Nonimmigrant Minorities." *Daedalus* 129: 233–59.

McGuire, W., C. McGuire, P. Child, and T. Fujoko. 1978. "Salience of Ethnicity in the Spontaneous Self-Concept as a Function of One's Ethnic Distinctiveness in the Social Environment." *Journal of Personality and Social Psychology* 36: 511–20.

Osborne, J. W. 1997. "Race and Academic Disidentification." *Journal of Educational Psychology* 89: 728–35.

———. 2001. "Testing Stereotype Threat: Does Anxiety Explain Race and Sex Differences in Achievement?" *Contemporary Educational Psychology* 26: 291–310.

Oyserman, D., K. Harrison, and D. Bybee. 2001. "Can Racial Identity Be Promotive of Academic Efficacy?" *International Journal of Behavioral Development* 25: 379–85.

Pinel, E. C. 1999. "Stigma Consciousness: The Psychological Legacy of Social Stereotypes." *Journal of Personality and Social Psychology* 76: 114–28.

Plaut, V. C. In press. "Cultural Models of Diversity: The Psychology of Difference and Inclusion." In *The Free Exercise of Culture: How Free Is It? How Free Ought It to Be?* ed. R. Shweder, M. Minow, and H. R. Markus. New York: Russell Sage Foundation.

Pronin, E., C. M. Steele, and L. Ross. 2001. *Stereotype Threat and the Feminine Identities of Women in Math.* Unpublished manuscript, Harvard University.

Purdie, V. J., C. M. Steele, P. G. Davies, and J. R. Crosby. 2001. *The Business of Diversity: Minority Trust within Organizational Cultures.* Presented at the annual meeting of the American Psychological Association. San Francisco, August.

Ramist, L., C. Lewis, and L. McCamley-Jenkins. 1994. *Student Group Differences in Predicting College Grades: Sex, Language, and Ethnic Groups* (College Board report no. 93–1, ETS no. 94.27). New York: College Entrance Examination Board.

Sartre, J. P. 1948. *Anti-Semite and Jew.* Trans. J. G. Becker. New York: Schocken Books.

Sekaquaptewa, D., and M. Thompson. In press. "The Differential Effects of Solo Status on Members of High and Low Status Groups." *Personality and Social Psychology Bulletin.*

Shih, M., T. L. Pittinsky, and N. Ambady. 1999. "Stereotype Susceptibility: Identity Salience and Shifts in Quantitative Performance." *Psychological Science* 10: 80–83.

Spencer, S. J., E. Iserman, P. G. Davies, and D. M. Quinn. 2001. *Suppression of Doubts, Anxiety, and Stereotypes as a Mediator of the Effect of Stereotype Threat on Women's Math Performance.* Unpublished manuscript, University of Waterloo.

Spencer, S. J., C. M. Steele, and D. M. Quinn. 1999. "Stereotype Threat and Women's Math Performance." *Journal of Experimental Social Psychology* 35: 4–28.

Stangor, C., C. Carr, and L. Kiang. 1998. "Activating Stereotypes Undermines Task Performance Expectations." *Journal of Personality and Social Psychology* 75: 1191–97.

Staples, B. 1994. *Parallel Time: Growing Up in Black and White.* New York; Pantheon Books.

Steele, C. M. 1975. "Name-Calling and Compliance." *Journal of Personality and Social Psychology* 31: 361–69.

———. 1992. "Race and the Schooling of Black Americans." *Atlantic Monthly* 269: 68–78.

———. 1997. "A Threat in the Air: How Stereotypes Shape Intellectual Identity and Performance." *American Psychologist* 52: 613–29.

———. 1999. "Thin Ice: Stereotype Threat and Black College Students." *Atlantic Monthly* 248: 44–54.

Steele, C. M., and J. Aronson. 1995. "Stereotype Threat and the Intellectual Test Performance of African Americans." *Journal of Personality and Social Psychology* 69: 797–811.

Steele, C. M., S. J. Spencer, and J. Aronson. 2002. "Contending with Group Image: The Psychology of Stereotype and Social Identity Threat." In *Advances in Experimental Social Psychology,* vol. 34, ed. M. Zanna. Academic Press.

Steele, C. M., S. J. Spencer, P. G. Davies, K. Harber, and R. E. Nisbett. 2001. *African*

American College Achievement: A "Wise" Intervention. Unpublished manuscript, Stanford University.

Steele, S. 1990. *The Content of Our Character: A New Vision of Race in America.* New York: St. Martin's.

Stone, J., C. I. Lynch, M. Sjomeling, and J. M. Darley. 1999. "Stereotype Threat Effects on Black and White Athletic Performance." *Journal of Personality and Social Psychology* 77: 1213–27.

Stricker, L. J. 1998. *Inquiring about Examinees' Ethnicity and Sex: Effects on AP Calculus AB Examination performance* (College Board report no. 98–1, ETS research report no. 98–5). New York: College Entrance Examination Board.

Taylor, D. M., S. C. Wright, F. M. Moghaddam, and R. Lalonde. 1990. "The Personal/Group Discrimination Discrepancy: Perceiving My Group, but Not Myself, to Be a Target for Discrimination." *Personality and Social Psychology Bulletin* 16: 254–62.

Tyler, T., P. Degoey, and H. Smith. 1996. "Understanding Why the Injustice of Group Procedures Matters: A Test of the Psychological Dynamics of the Group-Value Model." *Journal of Personality and Social Psychology* 70: 913–30.

Tyler, T., H. Smith, and Y. J. Huo. 1996. "Member Diversity and Leadership Effectiveness: Procedural Justice, Social Identity, and Group Dynamics." *Advances in Group Processes* 13: 33–66.

von Hippel, W., C. Hawkins, and J. W. Schooler. 2001. "Stereotype Distinctiveness: How Counterstereotypic Behavior Shapes the Self-Concept." *Journal of Personality and Social Psychology* 81: 193–205.

Wegner, D. M. 1994. "Ironic Processes of Mental Control." *Psychological Review* 101: 34–52.

Wenzlaff, R. M., and D. M. Wegner. 2000. "Thought Suppression." *Annual Review of Psychology* 51: 59–91.

Wheeler, S. C., W. B. Jarvis, and R. E. Petty. 2001. "Think unto Others: The Self-Destructive Impact of Negative Racial Stereotypes." *Journal of Experimental Social Psychology* 37: 173–80.

Wheeler, S. C., and R. E. Petty. 2001. "The Effects of Stereotype Activation on Behavior: A Review of Possible Mechanisms." *Psychological Bulletin* 127: 797–826.

Wolsko, C., B. Park, C. M. Judd., and B. Wittenbrink. 2000. "Framing Interethnic Ideology: Effects of Multicultural and Color-Blind Perspectives on Judgements of Groups and Individuals." *Journal of Personality and Social Psychology* 78: 635–54.

Hilliard / No Mystery: Closing the Achievement Gap between Africans and Excellence

Adger, Carolyn Temple, Donna Christian, and Orlando Taylor, eds. 1990. *Making the Connection: Language and Academic Achievement among African American Students.* McHenry, Ill.: Center for Applied Linguistics and Delta Systems.

Adler, Mortimer. 1982. *The Paidea Proposal: and Educational Manifesto.* New York: MacMillan.

Anderson, James. 1988. *The Education of Blacks in the South, 1860–1935.* Chapel Hill: University of North Carolina Press.

Asante, Molefi. 2000. *The Egyptian Philosophers: Ancient African Voices from Imhotep to Akhenaten.* Chicago: African American Images.

Backler, Alan, and S. Eakin. 1993. *Every Child Can Succeed.* Bloomington, Ind.: Agency for Instructional Technology.

Baratz, J. 1973. The relationship of Black English to Reading: Review of Research. In *Language Differences: Do They Interfere?* ed. J. Laffey and R. Shuy, pp. 101–13. Newark, N.J.: International Reading Association.

Barrett, Everard. 1992. "Teaching Mathematics through Context: Unleashing the Power of the Contextual Learner." In *Nurturing At-Risk Youth in Math and Science: Curriculum and Teaching Considerations.* Bloomington, Ind.: National Education Service.

Barzun, Jacques. 1965. *Race: A Study in Superstition.* New York: Harper Torchbooks.

Baugh, John. 1999. *Out of the Mouths of Slaves: African American Language and Educational Malpractice.* Austin: University of Texas Press.

Benedict, Ruth. 1959. *Race, Science, and Politics.* New York: Harper Torchbooks.

Berliner, David, and Bruce Biddle. 1996. *The Manufactured Crisis: Myths, Fraud, and the Attack on American Public Schools.* New York: Perseus Press.

Brewer, John. 1973. "Hidden Language: Ghetto Children Know What They're Talking About." In *Mother Wit from the Laughing Barrel,* ed. A. Dundees. Englewood Cliffs, N.J.: Prentice-Hall.

Carruthers, Jacob. 1995. *MDW NTR: Divine Speech, a Historical Reflection of African Deep Thought from the Time of the Pharaohs to the Present.* London: Karnak House.

College Board. 1983. *Academic Preparation for College: What Students Need to Know and Be Able to Do.* New York: The College Board.

Comer, James. 1980. *School Power.* New York: Free Press.

Crawford, Clinton, ed. 2001. *Ebonics and Language Education of African Ancestry Students.* New York: Sankofa World Publishers.

Dandy, Evelyn B. 1991. *Black Communications: Breaking Down the Barriers.* Chicago: African American Images.

Darling-Hammond, Linda. 2001. "New Standards and Old Inequalities: School Reform and the Education of African American Students." *Journal of Negro Education* 9 (4): 263–87.

Delpit, Lisa. 1995. *Other People's Children: Cultural Conflict in the Classroom.* New York: Morrow.

Diop, Cheikh Anta. 1991. *Civilization or Barbarism: An Authentic Anthropology.* New York: Lawrence Hill.

Donovan, M. Suzanne, and Cristopher K. Cross, eds. 2002. *Minority Students in Special and Gifted Education.* Washington, D.C.: Committee on Minority Representation in Special Education, Division of Behavioral and Social Sciences and Education, National Research Council, National Academy Press.

Dubois, Felix. 1969. *Timbuktu the Mysterious*. New York: Negro Universities Press.

Fairchild, Hal. 1991. "Scientific Racism: The Cloak of Objectivity." *Journal of Social Issues* 47 (3): 101–15.

Feuerstein, Reuven. 1980. *The Dynamic Assessment of Retarded Performers: The Learning Potential Assessment Device*. Baltimore: University Park Press.

Finch, Charles. 1998. *Star of Deep Beginnings: The Genesis of African Science and Technology*. Decatur, Ga.: Khenti.

Fordham, S., and J. Ogbu. 1986. "Black Students' School Success: Coping with the 'Burden of Acting White.'" *Urban Review* 18 (3): 176–203.

Foster, Michele. 1997. *Black Teachers on Teaching*. New York: New Press.

Gordon, Robert A. 1989. "Another View: Many Experts Do Support Shockley's Belief on the I.Q. Gap." *Baltimore Sun*, September 23.

Gossett, T. F. 1973. *Race: The History of an Idea in America*. New York: Schoken.

Gould, Stephen J. 1981. *The Mismeasure of Man*. New York: Norton.

Griaule, Marcel. 1986. *The Pale Fox*. Chino Valley, Ariz.: Continuum Foundation.

Guthrie, Robert. 1998. *Even the Rat Was White*. New York: Harper & Row.

Hale, Thomas A. 1998. "West Africa's Electric Educators." *Technos* 7 (14): 4.

Harkness, S., and C. M. Super. 1977. "Why African Children Are So Hard to Test." In *Annals of the New York Academy of Sciences*. Vol. 285, *Issues in Cross-Cultural Research*, ed. L. L. Adler, pp. 326–31. New York: New York Academy of Sciences.

Haycock, Katie. 1999. *Dispelling the Myth: High Poverty Schools Exceeding Expectations*. Washington, D.C.: Education Trust.

Heath, Shirley Brice. 1983. *Ways with Words*. Boston: Cambridge University Press.

Heller, Kirby, Wayne Holtzman, and Samuel Messick. 1982. *Placing Children in Special Education: A Strategy for Equity*. Washington, D.C.: National Academy Press.

Helms, Janet E. 1992. "Why Is There No Study of Cultural Equivalence in Standardized Cognitive Ability Testing?" *American Psychologist* 47: 1083–101.

Herrnstein, Richard, and Charles Murray. 1994. *The Bell Curve: Intelligence and Class Structure in American Life*. New York: Free Press.

Hilliard, Asa G., III. 1975. "The Strengths and Weaknesses of Cognitive Tests for Young Children." In *One Child Indivisible*, ed. J. D. Andrews. Washington, D.C.: National Association for the Education of Young Children.

———. 1983. "Psychological Factors Associated with Language in the Education of the African-American Child." *Journal of Negro Education* 52 (1): 24–34.

———. 1984. "I.Q. Testing as the Emperor's New Clothes: A Critique of Bias in Mental Testing." In *Perspective on Bias Mental Testing*, ed. Cecil Reynolds and Robert E. Brown, pp. 139–69. New York: Plenum Press.

———, ed. 1987. *Testing African American Students: Special Issue of the Negro Education Review* 38 (2 and 3). Also see reissue: 1995. Chicago: Third World Press.

———. 1988. "Misunderstanding and Testing Intelligence." In *Access to Knowledge*, ed. John Goodlad and Pamela Keating, pp. 145–57. Princeton, N.J.: College Entrance Examination Board.

———. 1990. "Back to Binet: The Case against the Use of IQ Tests in the Schools." *Contemporary Education* 61 (4): 184–89.

———. 1991. "Do We Have the Will to Educate All Children?" *Educational Leadership* 49 (1): 31–36.

———. 1994. "What Good Is This Thing Called Intelligence and Why Bother to Measure It?" *Journal of Black Psychology* 20 (4): 430–44.

———. 1995a. "Either a Paradigm Shift or No Mental Measurement: The Nonscience and Nonsense of *The Bell Curve.*" *Psych Discourse* 76 (10): 6–20.

———. 1995b. "Mathematical Excellence for Cultural Minority Students: What Is the Problem?" In *Prospects for School Mathematics: Seventy-five Years of Progress.* Reston, Virginia: National Council of Teachers of Mathematics.

———. 1998. *SBA: The Reawakening of the African Mind.* Gainesville, Fla.: Makare.

———. 2001. "Race, Identity, Hegemony, and Education: What Do We Need to Know Now? In *Race and Education: The Roles of History and Society in Educating African American Students,* ed. William Watkins, James Lewis, and Victoria Chou, pp. 7–33. Boston: Allyn & Bacon.

Hilliard, Asa G., III, and Barbara Sizemore, eds. 1984. *Saving the African American Child: A Report of the National Alliance of Black School Educators, Inc., Task Force on Black Academic and Cultural Excellence.* Washington, D.C.: National Alliance of Black School Educators.

Hilliard, Constance, ed. 1998. *Intellectual Traditions of Pre-colonial Africa.* New York: McGraw Hill.

Hoover, M., R. L. Politzer, and D. Taylor. 1987. "Bias in Reading Tests for Black Language Speakers: A Sociolinguistic Perspective." *Negro Educational Review* 38 (2 and 3): 81–99.

Houts, Paul, ed. 1977. *The Myth of Measurability.* New York: Hart.

Howard, Jeffrey, and Ray Hammond. 1985. "Rumors of Inferiority." *New Republic,* September 9, 18–23.

Hughes, Mary F. 1995. *Achieving Despite Diversity: Why Are Some Schools Successful in Spite of the Obstacles They Face? A Study of the Characteristics of Effective and Less Effective Elementary Schools in West Virginia Using Qualitative and Quantitative Methods.* Charleston: West Virginia Education Fund.

Hunt, C. Helm. 2000. *High Poverty, High Achievement: Kentucky Schools Are Proving That Success Is Possible for All Students.* Associate Commissioner Kentucky Department of Education.

Hunwick, John. 1999. *Timbuktu and the Sonhay Empire: Al Sa'di's Ta'rikh al Sudan Down to 1613 and Other Contemporary Documents.* London: Brill.

IROA Newsletter. 1997. "Low Income Does Not Cause Low School Achievement: Creating a Sense of Family and Respect in the School Environment." *IROA Newsletter,* June-July Intercultural Development Research Association, 5835 Callaghan Road, Suite 350, San Antonio, TX, 78228–1190; (210) 684-8180; www.iora.org.

Jacobs, Paul. 1977. *Up the IQ.* New York: Wyden.

Jensen, A. 1980. *Bias in Mental Testing.* New York: Free Press.

Jones, Faustine. 1991. "Urban Schools That Work." *Journal of Negro Education*, special edition 57 (3).

———. 1981. *A Traditional Model of Education Excellence: Dunbar High School of Little Rock, Arkansas.* Washington, D.C.: Howard University Press.

Jones, J. Arthur. 1990. "Look at Math Teachers, Not 'Black English.'" In *Essays and Policy Studies.* Washington, D.C.: Institute for Independent Education.

Jones, R., ed. 1996. *Handbook of Tests and Measurement for Black Populations.* Cobb & Henry.

Joseph, George Gheverghse. 2000. *The Crest of the Peacock: Non-European Roots of Mathematics.* Princeton, N.J.: Princeton University Press.

Kamin, Leon. 1974. *The Science and Politics of I.Q.* New York: Wiley.

Kozol, Jonathan. 1991. *Savage Inequalities: Children in America's Schools.* New York: Crown.

Labov, W. 1970. "The Logic of Non-standard English." In *Language and Poverty,* ed. F. Williams, pp. 153–89. Chicago: Markham.

Ladefoged, Peter. 1968. *A Phonetic Study of West African Languages: An Auditory Instrumental Study.* Cambridge: Cambridge University Press.

Ladson-Billings, Gloria. 1994. *The Dreamkeepers: Successful Teaching of African American Children.* San Francisco: Jossey-Bass.

Landis, D., P. McGrew, H. Day, J. Savage, and T. Saral. 1976. "Word Meaning in Black and White." In *Variations in Black and White: Conditions of the Social Environment,* ed. H. C. Triandis. Urbana: University of Illinois Press.

Levine, Daniel U., and Lawrence Lezotte. 1990. *Unusually Effective Schools.* Madison, Wis.: National Center for Effective Schools Research and Development, University of Wisconsin.

Mathews, Jay. 1992. "Escalante Still Stands and Delivers: A Great Math Teacher Tackles New Problems." *Newsweek,* July 20, pp. 58–59.

McDougall, Christopher. 1999. "Trial with Fire: Students Draw from Their Troubled Lives to Bring Street Wisdom to Jurisprudence." *New York Times,* August 1, pp. 33–34.

Montague, Ashley. 1974. *Man's Most Dangerous Myth: The Fallacy of Race.* New York: Oxford University Press.

Mufwene, Salikoko S., John T. Rickford, Guy Balley, and John Baugh. 1998. *African-American English: Structure, History, and Use.* New York: Routledge.

Ngubane, Jordon K. 1979. *Conflict of Minds: Changing Power Distributions in South Africa.* New York: Books in Focus.

Nobles, Wade. 1987. "Psychometrics and African-American reality: A Question of Cultural Antimony." *Negro Educational Review* 38 (2 and 3): 45–55. See also Hilliard, Asa G., III, ed. 1995. *Testing African American Students.* Chicago: Third World Press.

Obenga, Theophile. 1995. *A Lost Tradition: African Philosophy in World History.* Philadelphia: Source Editions.

Orr, Eleanor. 1987. *Twice as Less: Black English and the Performance of Black Students in Mathematics and Science.* New York: Norton.

Perkins, Susan. 1999. *Kentucky Elementary School Performance and Poverty.* Lexington, Ky.: Prichard Committee for Academic Excellence (Prichard Committee for Academic Excellence, 99 Citizen and Parent Volunteers, Robert F. Sexton, Executive Director).

Perry, Theresa, and Lisa Delpit, eds. 1998. *The Real Ebonics Debate: Power, Language, and the Education of African-American Children.* Boston: Beacon Press.

Peshkin, Alan. 2001. *Permissible Advantage: The Moral Consequences of Elite Schooling.* Mahwah, N.J.: Erlbaum.

Phillips, Carol Bunson. 1979. *Afro-American Culture/Cognition.*

Ramirez, David J., Terrence G. Wiley, Gerda de Klerk, and Enid Lee. 2000. *Ebonics in the Urban Education Debate.* Long Beach, Calif.: Center for Language Minority Education and Research.

Reitman, Valerie. 1994. "Tots Do Swimmingly in Language-Immersion Programs." *Wall Street Journal,* February 15, pp. B1–10.

Rickford, John Russell, and Russel John Rickford. 2000. *Spoken Soul: The Story of Black English.* New York: Wiley.

Rowe, Helga M., ed. 1991. *Intelligence: Reconceptualization and Measurement.* Hillsdale, N.J.: Erlbaum.

Saad, Elias. 1983. *The Social History of Timbuktu: The Role of Muslim Scholars and Notables, 1400–1900.* New York: Cambridge University Press.

Saunders, William L., and J. C. Rivers. 1996. *Cumulative and Residual Effects of Teachers on Future Student Academic Achievement: Value Added Research and Assessment.* Knoxville: University of Tennessee.

Schmoker, Mike. 1999. *Results: The Keys to Continuous School Improvement.* Arlington, Va.: Association for Supervision and Curriculum Development.

Shade, Barbara, ed. 1997. *Culture, Style, and Educative Process: Making Schools Work for Racially Diverse Students.* Springfield, Ill. Thomas.

Sizemore, Barbara. 1988. *The Algebra of African-American Achievement. Effective Schools: Critical Issues in the Education of Black Children.* Washington, D.C.: National Alliance of Black School Educators.

Sizemore, Barbara, Carlos Brosard, and Berny Harrigan. 1994. *An Abashing Anomaly: The High Achieving Predominately Black Elementary Schools.* Pittsburgh, Pa.: University of Pittsburgh Press.

Skutnabb-Kangas, Tove. 2000. *Linguistic Genocide in Education or Worldwide Diversity and Human Rights.* Mahway, N.J.: Erlbaum.

Smith, E. 1978. "The Retention of the Phonological, Phonemic, and Morphophonemic Features of Africa in Afro-American Ebonics." Fullerton, Calif.: seminar paper 43, Department of Linguistics, California State University, Fullerton.

Smitherman, Geneva. 1977. *Talkin' and Testifyin': The Language of Black America.* Boston: Houghton Mifflin.

———. 2000. *Talkin' That Talk: Language, Culture, and Education in African America.* New York: Routledge.

Snyderman, Mark, and Stanley Rothman. 1988. *The I.Q. Controversy: The Media and Public Policy.* New Brunswick, N.J. Transaction.

Suzuki, Sinichi. 1984. *Nurtured by Love: The Classic Approach to Talent Education.* Smithtown, N.Y.: Exposition Press.

Turner, L. 1969. *Africanism in the Gullah Dialect.* New York: Arno Press.

Van Keulen, G., G. Weddington, and C. DeBose. 1998. *Speech, Language, Learning, and the African-American Child.* Boston: Allyn & Bacon.

Vass, W. K. 1974. *The Bantu Speaking Heritage of the United States.* Los Angeles: Center for Afro-American Studies, University of California.

Washington Post, 1991. "Dialects of Blacks, Whites Veer Apart, Which May Speak Poorly for the Future." *Atlanta Journal and Constitution,* April 30.

Watson, C., and G. Smitherman. 1996. *Educating African American Males: Detroit's Malcolm X Academy Solution.* Chicago: Third World Press.

Webber, Thomas L. 1978. *Deep Like the Rivers: Education in the Slave Community, 1831–1865.* New York: Norton.

Weinberg, Meyer. 1977. *A Chance to Learn: The History of Race and Education in the United States.* New York: Cambridge University Press.

Williams, Robert L. 1975. *Ebonics: The True Language of Black Folks.* St. Louis, Mo.: Institute of Black Studies.

Wilson, Amos. 1990. *Awakening the Natural Genius of Black Children.* New York: Afrikan World Infosystems.

Wong, Edward. 2000. "Poorest Schools Lack Teachers and Computers." *New York Times,* August 13.

Yee, Al H. 1983. "Ethnicity and Race: Psychological Perspectives." *Educational Psychologist* 18 (1): 14–24.

Yee, A. H., H. H. Fairchild, F. Weizmann, and Gail E. Wyatt. 1993. "Addressing Psychology's Problems with Race." *American Psychologist* 48 (11): 32–40.